The Non-Boring Safe Travel Guide

More Non-Boring Travel Guides

**The Non-Boring Vacation Packing Guide:
Save Your Back, Time, and Money**

**The Non-Boring Travel Money Guide:
Dollars, Rupiah and Sense**
(coming soon)

The Non-Boring Safe Travel Guide

Travel Safety Tips & Travel Health Advice

ELISABETH SOWERBUTTS

www.NonBoringTravelGuides.com

First Print Edition September, 2012

Also available as an eBook

ISBN: 978-1479141692

Published by *Non-Boring Travel Guides*
www.nonBoringTravelGuides.com

Disclaimer

This book contains information regarding travel health and safety that is the author's own opinions and experiences. It is published for general reference, entertainment and travel dreaming purposes only and is not intended to be a substitute for independent medical advice by a professional medical practitioner. The author disclaims any personal liability, for the information contained within.

If you have specific health issues, seek medical advice. Medical practitioners spent years in school learning this stuff, the author did not.

The author has made every effort to ensure the accuracy and completeness of the information contained within, she assumes no responsibility for errors, inaccuracies, omissions or inconsistencies.

CONTENTS

Part 3:
Traveling Safely: Traffic, Petty Theft & Terrorism

Afterword
When Going Home Feels Wrong

INTRODUCTION OR WHY I WROTE THIS BOOK

This is the bit where I'm supposed to say I'm a medical professional, with a particular research interest in travel. Or maybe I've run security for a large international firm for a decade or so.

Well, no.

I have a particular interest in travel, true, but I have no medical qualifications at all and my first aid certificate is lapsed. I've never done security, unless you count the couple of times that single guys have asked me to accompany them to the red light districts of Sydney and Bangkok, so they wouldn't get hit on so much. No, it didn't work, but we got some interesting offers for "couple shows".

So don't use this book as medical advice. It's not, if you want proper medical advice, go to a medical practitioner; you'll undoubtedly find one quite close to where you live.

What I can offer you, dear reader, is a compendium of travel experience and common sense developed over 30 years of independent travel, during which I've travelled to over 55 countries. I've yet to get seriously ill, assaulted or even killed from traveling. And my experience is pretty typical.

Which is not to say I've travelled incident free. I was hit by a London cab, it wasn't the cabbie's fault – I walked out in front of him, after looking the wrong way, as I was used to the traffic being on the other side of the road. I was lucky to limp away from the scene with just a badly bruised foot. I've nearly drowned, once in a bad off-shore rip in Mexico, when I didn't know the Spanish word for "dangerous" (*peligroso*, if you are wondering). I had my wallet pick-pocketed on an Indian train losing about US$20. A moment's carelessness saw my day pack in Bolivia disappear, along with a camera and more importantly, an irreplaceable film. I've also travelled in countries during major riots (England and Peru) and dodged a revolution in Nepal. All of these incidents occurred when I was traveling as a solo woman. So, I have some great travel stories and a far more realistic view of the "dangerous" world, than you will find on your TV. The world is a wonderful and in general, safe place. Particularly if you pack your common sense with you.

Because, and Fox News won't tell you this, the world is full of good people. They may be a different color from you and they may not speak English, but very little of the world is out to get you.

This book is aimed at the independent leisure traveler. If you are traveling with a tour group for the entire time, I would expect that they would help if you ended up sick. But there are still issues you will want to consider. And maybe I can persuade you that you don't need the security of a tour group next time.

If you haven't travelled much or are heading to your first non-first world destination, then you may be concerned about coming in contact with exotic diseases, getting food poisoning or being a victim of terrorism.

The chance of getting the exotic disease or experiencing the terrorism are as good as winning the lotto. Food poisoning you may well get, but it's unlikely to be serious. According to the WHO, the number one killer of healthy Americans traveling abroad is motor vehicle accidents.
http://wwwnc.cdc.gov/travel/yellowbook/2012/chapter–2-the-pre-travel-consultation/injuries-and-safety.htm

Surprised? Thought so. Our 24/7 media-rich world assaults us with stories of murder, mayhem and dangers from across the world, but coming home safe and uninjured is not really a news story. So the myth of the dangerous world is perpetuated.

I hope that some of my experiences will help inform you and therefore make your travel safe and healthy. However, the Universe has a sense of humor – you can take every precaution mentioned in this and every other travel book and still end up sick and injured. Sorry, there are no guarantees. I just want to increase your odds and reduce your worries. (Or, quite probably more importantly, the worries of your friends and relatives). Or maybe I will make the boring delay at the airport a little less dull.

Whichever, I'll have achieved my purpose.

I've split this book into three sections. Of them all the first one, pre-trip preparations, is probably the most important. The next two sections talk about staying healthy on the road and staying safe. Finally I talk about that sad moment when you return home.

Elisabeth Sowerbutts
Wellington, N.Z.
2012

Part 1
Pre-Trip Health And
Safety Tips

"An ounce of prevention is worth a pound of cure."

—Benjamin Franklin

INTRODUCTION: PRE-TRIP HEALTH AND SAFETY TIPS

When people get into trouble overseas it's usually purely from a lack of planning and lack of knowledge. It has never been easier to find up-to-date information on your destination before you leave home. But it also seems people have never been lazier. Personally I love travel planning, second only to travel itself. But even if you are not a planner there really are a few things you need to check out before hopping on that plane!

Just as you wouldn't head overseas without a current passport with at least six months to run before expiry, you also shouldn't leave home without some basic research about the health risks of the area you're traveling and any potential safety issues.

A little bit of pre-trip research will tell you what to take and manage to avoid such travel *faux pas* as arriving in the middle of the monsoon season or not realizing that it gets cold enough to snow in northern Vietnam's winter.

So let's talk about what you should be doing before you set foot on that plane:

- Vaccinations and which health supplies are worth carrying.

- Travel insurance:– health and evacuation.

- Travel safety warnings:– what your government is telling you and what to believe.

- Mental preparations:– yup, it may all be in your mind!

GETTING IN SHAPE FOR TRAVEL

Okay, if you are just going to spend a couple of weeks on a beach, you can probably skip this section. But if you are traveling for a month or more, I seriously suggest you read it!

SORT OUT YOUR BODY BEFORE YOU LEAVE

Going from sitting in front of the computer all day in an office, to out and about sight-seeing may result in you finding that you are a little unfit. Just walking a museum in Europe can take eight hours and be surprisingly tiring (marble floors are *very* unforgiving on leg muscles). I'm not saying you need to start getting fit before you leave, I'm just saying it will hurt less if you do, particularly if you are over 30. Trust me on this!

Health Checkup

If you have a long-term illness or condition then talk to your doctor. It's well worth having a note from him describing your condition in medical terms, so that if the worst happens you can pass this on to local medical staff. If you are traveling with someone you should also make sure they are aware of any symptoms and know what to do in an emergency. Even if you are in good health, having a checkup before you go on a longer trip is a good idea.

If you never trek at high altitude, go deep-sea diving or bungee jumping normally, then it might be a good idea to talk to your doctor to see if your condition could be a problem while doing any of these. For example, I'm extremely myopic (short-sighted) and only recently discovered that this means that I should not bungee jump as the risk of a detached retina is lot higher for those of us who can't see their hand in front of their face.

Prescription Drugs

If you are on essential drugs then make sure know how long you can go without those drugs, if the worst happens and you lose them. If you are traveling with someone else – make sure they carry some of your drugs (and you, theirs, if necessary).

If you do need to carry quantities of prescription drugs, they are easier to pack if they are in foil packs rather than in plastic containers and obviously become less bulky as the trip progresses.

If you are on any regular prescriptions get a copy of the prescription – if you lose your pills, you should be able to replace them in most places. However, brand names vary from country to country, so make sure your doctor gives you a written list that includes common generic names.

If you need your pills don't pack them in any bag you are checking in, make sure they are in your carry-on bag.

Dental

Obviously it makes a difference if you are traveling for a few weeks or a year or more but I would suggest that you have a dental checkup if you haven't had one for a while. Routine dentistry is generally not covered by travel insurance and you don't want to waste travel time on a trip to the dentist! There is also a law of nature that says if a filling is about to fall out, it will do so when you are eating some new and exciting cuisine in an exotic locale.

Eyes

If you have glasses or contacts make sure you have a copy of your prescription with you. If you are so blind you can't function without your glasses, carrying a spare pair or contacts is a wise precaution. I once lost my glasses during a mishap river tubing. I'd left my main bag in a different town and I had to survive another couple of days and take a bus back to my base. All without being able to see much beyond my out-stretched arm. It wasn't a lot of fun and I've never been separated from my spare pair of glasses since. Even if they are an old prescription they are a lot better than nothing.

I wouldn't necessarily buy another set of glasses or contacts before traveling. In many parts of the world, particularly Asia and India, glasses and contacts are a LOT cheaper than in the West. Take the opportunity to have some spares made.

Even if you always wear contacts – take glasses as well. You shouldn't wear contacts on a flight over about three hours (the dry, low-pressure cabin will affect the contacts and cause irritation). And you may have unexpected problems in areas with lots of dust or pollution. Plus, if you are trekking or camping where it's hard to clean your hands you don't want to be handling contacts.

RESEARCH YOUR DESTINATION

How long you travel is just as important as where you are going. Pretty much the hierarchy of countries where you may get seriously ill are as follows:

- North America / Western Europe / Australia / Japan / Korea / Singapore / New Zealand
- Eastern Europe / Malaysia / Chile / Argentina / Pacific Islands
- the rest of South America / Central America / SE Asia / China / South Africa
- India / Nepal / Middle East / Northern Africa
- sub-Saharan Africa (excluding South Africa)

Yes, I know, it's a gross generalization, but it's just silly to assume that that the risks of staying in Western Europe are comparable to those of rural China. At one stage when I lived in London, every second person I knew who came back from an overland African truck trip ended up with some exotic intestinal wildlife. Not nice.

If you are traveling for more than a month in hot, humid, developing nations, particularly in Africa, you are far more likely to end up with some strange disease than if you spend two weeks on a bus tour of Australia or Europe. It's just a fact of life that some nasty diseases are spread much more easily in hot humid conditions than in cooler or dryer climates. If the country doesn't have good sanitation and public health standards, then the longer you are exposed the more likely you are to pick up something.

In addition, if you are working or volunteering on farms, living in villages and working with local children and animals then you are more likely to be exposed to more exotic diseases than a backpacker who is moving from one backpacker hang out to the next. If you are sticking to the big cities of Asia – your chances of getting something you couldn't get at home is pretty limited. However as soon as you start traveling in the countryside and staying in villages, home stays or local hotels, then your disease risk increases dramatically.

But that's an average. One of my worst cases of food poisoning was in Australia and I was never sick during long trips in Egypt, Syria or Turkey. Things can escalate quite quickly. I got food poisoning in Nepal but went trekking anyway – because I was well enough to be bored hanging around the hotel and my friends were all leaving. I kept up, just, but I was still a bit weak. I didn't eat enough because after food poisoning, I tend to get really picky about food and there weren't a lot of options in the tea-houses we were staying at. All of this was pure nuisance value only, except the following day, there was snow on a high pass and I was walking alone because I was still slow. I got scared – it was white-out conditions and I was worried about missing the path. I rushed and fell hard on one of my knees. I made it through the storm but was laid up with a very sore knee for a day or so. I recovered and completed the trek. About eight years later I was diagnosed with osteo-arthritis in that very same knee. It's a pain to this day and I suspect it all happened because I was out trekking when maybe I should have stayed a few more days in a comfortable guest house in Kathmandu.

Vaccinations? Yes!

I'm not debating whether or not you should have vaccinations – there are a few that are arguable — but the core vaccinations are non-negotiable. Some people in the West seem to have forgotten that we are only a few generations away from TB and diphtheria being major causes of death. I met someone who had Hepatitis in South America—he was about 30, but looked and moved like an old man. Some things are just not worth the risk.

Travel medicine is a medical specialism: go to a specialist travel clinic to get your shots and advice. They will have the current World Health Organization

(WHO) list of recommended and required vaccinations for every country in the world. Allow plenty of time, some vaccinations need more than one jab, spread over weeks. Some shots will leave you with a sore arm and feeling a little unwell for the rest of the day - and some take some weeks to become fully effective.

Make sure you ask them to issue you the "Yellow Card". The International Vaccination Yellow Card (*Carte Jaune*) is issued by the WHO and is an international certificate of vaccination. It is not just a useful record of your vaccinations but is required proof of vaccination for Yellow Fever which is required by some countries in Africa and South America before you're be allowed to enter.

Compulsory Vaccinations for Developing Countries

It is rare for a vaccination to be compulsory but yellow fever is for parts of Africa and South America. Meningitis is compulsory for travel to Saudi Arabia during the Haj.

Highly Recommended Vaccinations

Be up to date on your tetanus, diphtheria, measles, mumps, rubella, TB shots and polio vaccine (which is my favorite because it's a sugar cube, not an injection).

These diseases are far more common in the developing world than in the West. They are serious diseases that can make you very unwell, permanently physically disabled, mentally impaired and may even be fatal. A flu shot is also generally recommended. Even if you are traveling at home, these are routine shots that everyone should have.

Tetanus a.k.a. "lock jaw" is another must-have, even if you are not traveling. Most adults need a booster every 10 years or so. Tetanus is spread by contaminated manure and soil and any small cut or abrasion can become infected.

Recommended Vaccinations for Most Non-Western Countries

Hepatitis A is transmitted via contaminated food and water. Hepatitis B is transmitted from bodily fluids and blood.

Within the last 10 years a reliable effective vaccine has become available for Hepatitis A and B. If you have both shots within six months immunity lasts at least 30 years, probably for life. Hepatitis is a nasty disease which can make you ill for up to six months, can permanently damage the liver and which can prevent you from drinking alcohol for at least six months. It is well worth avoiding.

You may have noticed that I made no comment about those who refuse vaccinations, that's because if you don't want to get vaccinated, you should probably stay home. Vaccinations work and their use has saved countless thousands of lives.

MOSQUITOES: ANNOYING AND DANGEROUS

Mosquitoes are not just an annoyance: they can be fatal in some parts of the world, as they carry both malaria and dengue fever. In certain countries and times of the year, they can also carry Japanese Encephalitis and Ross River virus.

Anti-Malarials

Anti-malarials are however far more problematic. As is some of the advice that you will be given. I've been advised, for example, that I should take anti-malarials for southern Thailand and yet in the dry season there are no mosquitoes to be seen.

Malaria is endemic to large parts of the tropical world. Mosquito numbers and hence your chances of getting bitten vary a lot by season. Mosquitoes breed in still water, so the wet season is worse, as is anywhere in the jungle and near water. I personally never stay anywhere that describes the accommodation as being "near a lagoon".

There is no vaccination for malaria but you can take prophylactic drugs which reduce (effectively to zero) the chance of getting the fatal form of cerebral malaria. Unfortunately they are not 100% effective on non-fatal varieties of malaria. They all also have side-effects, which can be severe and range from stomach upsets to body aches, bizarre dreams, paranoia and sensitivity to sunlight. For some people the side-effects are worse than the disease.

What isn't negotiable is that, if you are going to take the risk, you need to avoid being bitten by mosquitoes. If you are in an area with dengue fever or Ross River virus (Asia, Pacific Islands, northern Australia) you will need to do this anyway as there is nothing to take against these diseases.

AVOIDING BEING BITTEN

There is no cure or preventative for dengue fever. Instead you should try the following, remembering that dengue-bearing mosquitoes tend to bite during the day, while their malarial-carrying cousins bite at sunset and night. Plus getting badly bitten is really uncomfortable as the bites will often get infected in tropical climates.

Some of us are more susceptible to bites or maybe react more to them, but all of the following will help:

- Sleeping in an air-conditioned room.

- Sleeping under a mosquito net.

- Wearing insect repellent containing at least 30% DEET.

- Wearing long sleeves and trousers, especially in the evening around sun set.

- Wearing light colored clothing (mosquitoes are attracted by dark colored clothing).

- Wearing Permethrin-treated clothing will kill mosquitoes and the chemical remains effective for approximately six months.

TRAVEL MEDICINE RESOURCES

For further information and specific country information, which changes quite frequently, I refer you to the following official websites:

For USA: CDC Travel Clinics

http://wwwnc.cdc.gov/travel/page/travel-clinics.htm

For the UK: FCO Health Advice

http://www.fco.gov.uk/en/travel-and-living-abroad/staying-safe/health/

WHAT HEALTH SUPPLIES YOU SHOULD PACK AND WHAT YOU CAN LEAVE AT HOME

I travel light, very light, carry-on luggage only usually; which is not to say there are not some health supplies that I don't always have with me. Remember, any liquids you carry on to the plane must be in containers of less than 100ml (3oz).

SUNTAN LOTION

Common problems on holiday have to do with too much sun and too much booze. Particularly if you are hitting the beaches somewhere warmer don't under-estimate just how much damage the sun can do to you. Fall asleep for a few hours on an Australian beach and you will wake up in hospital with third degree burns and possible sun stroke. Good quality, waterproof, suntan lotion can be expensive but it's essential. It's one of the few things that can be cheaper at home than in most of the developing world. SPF30 is usually recommended for fair skins.

DEET-RICH INSECT REPELLENT (30%)

I hope I've convinced you that being bitten by mosquitoes is worth avoiding. This is not a time to worry about going organic. I can 100% assure you that citronella smells nice but does nothing to repel mosquitoes. If desperate, cigarettes work well, it's the smoke. Personally, I stick with the DEET and wash my hands well before touching any plastic, like a laptop or cell phone. Bonus: it will protect you against plenty of biting insects apart from mosquitoes.

TRAVEL SOCKS FOR LONG HAUL: FLIGHTS, BUSES, TRAINS

These can be a life saver, as the help reduce the chance of getting deep vein thrombosis (DVT), a potentially fatal condition where blood clots lodge in your body's organs. They are highly recommended for any long-haul (over four hours) flights. But more people probably get blood clots from long car or bus journeys (trains are better, as you can get up and walk around easily). The socks take up little space and are particularly recommended for anyone who has one of the risk factors (including high blood pressure, recent surgery or pregnancy).

ORAL RE-HYDRATION MIXTURE

If you do get food poisoning it's rarely ever more than a few hours of unpleasantness. What you do need to be careful of is not getting dehydrated. A medically sound re-hydration mixture is 1/2 teaspoon of salt and 6 teaspoons of sugar in 1 liter (quart) of water. Proper dehydration mixture, which you can get in small packets, takes up hardly any space and will taste a LOT better, which is important if you feel nauseous.

CONTRACEPTION

If you are a guy you can skip right on to the next section, although taking some decent-quality condoms from home may be a good idea... If you are on a contraceptive pill, although you can buy them anywhere in the world, it might be worth bringing enough of the type you are used to with you. If that sounds like too much hassle, then there are other long-term contraceptive options, including patches and other devices. But, if you are going to change, make sure you do this a few months before you travel to make sure it works for you.

Even if you aren't planning on using oral contraceptives for their stated purpose, I travelled for years using the pill to control my periods. It made them much lighter and almost pain free – again worth considering.

While we are talking ladies only, I'd suggest bringing some tampons along. They are not always available everywhere and given that most stores are NOT self-service, fairly embarrassing to ask for, particularly with a language barrier and with predominately male shop assistants (don't think I need to draw the picture!).

RECOMMENDED FIRST AID KIT

In addition to the above I carry:

- Voltaren: anti-inflammatory useful for muscle aches and pains.

- Panadol/Aspirin or other pain relief.

- Antihistamine tablets: useful for treating colds, allergies and motion sickness.

- SeaLegs: motion sickness medicine - I get easily and badly seasick. If you are not prone, the antihistamine will do the same job.

- Cold Relief Capsules: due to exposure to foreign bugs, there is a good chance that you will get a cold at some point during your travels. Having a few cold relief capsules handy is always a good idea. If the capsules also induce drowsiness (think Nyquil), then the pills can also be used to aid sleeping.

- A variety of different-shaped plasters.

- Gel-based second skin: if I'm worried about blisters and planning on doing some serious hiking.

- Anti-Itch Cream: when you're traveling, there are many new things that may cause your skin to itch, bug bites being especially common. An anti-itch cream such as hydrocortisone will help to relieve you in this department.

- Tweezers: good for getting things out of your body, like splinters or hairs that are growing in the wrong place.

- Nail scissors: though you will lose these if you pack them in carry-on luggage, alternatively buy a pair on arrival as they are very useful

- Needles: with thread for sewing broken clothes, but the needle, if sterilized in a flame, is useful for removing debris from wounds, as well

- Safety Pins: useful for holding things together. Again take no space and are probably more useful on clothes than bandages.

I've never used the following but they take up no space and I could use them if needed:

- Non-adherent absorbent dressing.

- Sterile water wipe towel.

- Emergency burn care oil (Tea Tree Oil). The best treatment for any burn is to hold it under cold running water for about 10 minutes, but this would help afterwards.

All of the above fits into a 15x10cm (6"x4") zipped plastic pouch, which I probably got as part of a cosmetic giveaway at some time. It's clear which makes

31

it easier to identify in the bottom of the pack. It weighs under 100g (3.5oz) and I include a couple of tiny spools of thread so it doubles as my sewing kit as well. Don't use a rigid box – it takes up too much space.

WHAT YOU DON'T NEED TO BRING

I never carry antibiotics for stomach upsets, there is a growing, world-wide problem with increased antibiotic resistance. Plus, they won't work on all forms of food poisoning. Oral re-hydration mixture, on the other hand, will..

A mosquito net. Really, you do not need to bring one! Unless you are camping that is. If you are staying in accommodation, however cheap, if you need mosquito nets, they will be provided. Some Duct tape to repair the holes in the supplied net may be useful, but otherwise, no, you really don't need one.You can get combined insect repellent and suntan lotion but even as bite-prone as I am, I often don't need to have both on at the same time, so it's not really worth it.

An expensive, branded medical kit. Most of them have a whole lot of stuff you don't need or don't know how to use. Create one of your own and take only what you will use..

Also don't pack lozenges for coughs if traveling somewhere warm, they melt quite easily and make an awful mess. You can buy something to suck on almost anywhere. Ditto with cough syrup – it's just too messy.

HEALTH INSURANCE: WHAT'S COVERED, WHAT'S NOT

Yes I mean health insurance not travel insurance. Travel insurance will cover you for absolutely everything and maybe one day I will get kidnapped or die and regret not getting paid out the $250,000 for the inconvenience. Probably not.

I've lost items several times through theft, both times it was a genuine claim, neither time would the company pay out. It wasn't worth pushing it. And, no, they won't cover you for the $1000 your camera actually cost – it's more like the $200 they think it's worth now, because it was a couple of years old!

Buy travel insurance or not, as you wish, but what's important is health insurance and medical evacuation insurance.

I've never needed travel health insurance but I've seen enough tourists get run over, fall off motor-bikes or get really sick, to think it would be quite nice to have a number to call collect and have someone else to pick up the bills.

DO YOU NEED TO BUY TRAVEL HEALTH INSURANCE?

Sometimes, though, you may not need it.

If you are traveling somewhere that has a reciprocal agreement you will already be covered: Australians have automatic coverage in New Zealand and New Zealanders are covered in Ireland. European union residents are covered in other EU countries.

If you need health insurance for the countries you are traveling to then check your current health insurance, if any, it may cover you for overseas travel, sometimes for an extra fee.

WHAT'S THE BEST POLICY?

The one that's there for you when you need it; i.e., not necessarily the cheapest. When choosing a company here are some benefits you may have thought were standard, but are not:

- A number you can call collect (not just a free call number, they don't work overseas) 24/7; accidents are no respecters of office hours.

- Concierge service, which will help with local translations and medical advice as required.

- Unlimited claims on medical expenses.

34

- Medical evacuation: this may be a separate insurance, but if you are traveling in places like Africa or Myanmar, you probably want to be evacuated not treated in the local hospital. In contrast, Malaysia, Thailand and the Philippines have developed medical tourism industries where local hospitals may provide better care than those at home.

- Coverage for someone to accompany you home, particularly if you are traveling solo. It could be more than nice to have a friend or relative fly out to escort you.

COVER FOR IMPERFECT HEALTH: PRE-EXISTING CONDITIONS

Getting travel insurance if you have a pre-existing condition is not necessarily a lost cause, but you need to be careful. In general, travel insurance won't cover you for health conditions that you already have. Sometimes it doesn't matter; I've had osteo-arthritis in my knees for years but there is no risk that tomorrow I'm going to wake up and not get out of bed, regardless of whether I'm overseas or not! On the other hand, if you have any heart-related issues, you will probably want travel insurance to cover.

The key is to understand what you are and are not covered for. If in doubt, assume you have no coverage. In some cases, common or minor conditions, such as controlled high-blood pressure or asthma, will be covered as long as you declare it when you buy the policy. Get anything you agree on with your insurance company in writing.

You need to make an informed decision as to whether or not you have or indeed need, insurance coverage for a particular condition.

Also, check cover if you are pregnant; insurance won't cover you later in your pregnancy for obvious reasons!

My best advice is to shop around. In my partner's case, I got a whole range of answers as to whether he'd be covered while traveling, from "no" to "maybe". "Maybe" turned into "yes" after we provided a specialist's report saying that he was medically fit to travel.

If you do have less than perfect health, you should arrange your travel insurance as soon as possible. It can take weeks to do if you need specialist reports; this may even be before you book the trip. Ideally as soon as you pay deposits or start booking non-refundable flights and accommodation, get your insurance. Then, if something happens before you start the trip, you are covered.

WHEN WILL YOU NOT BE COVERED?

Be very clear as to what is and is not covered by your health insurance. For example, travel insurance is designed for travel: if you are volunteering or working you may need to tell your insurance company. Also, make sure you know what is and is not a "dangerous activity" and therefore excluded. Skiing, scuba diving, water-skiing, motorbike riding and even hiking can all come under some companies' definitions of dangerous. Be on the safe side and get written confirmation from them that they will cover your proposed activities.

The biggest issue to avoid, though, is lying to your company, even by omission. If you have a medical condition, tell them. Yes, they won't check when you take out the policy, but they most certainly will if you claim and deny your claim, even if you forgot to mention your ulcers and the claim was actually a broken arm. In fact, the safest option is to send the company a complete set of your medical records. They don't want you to do that, because then they can't say you didn't tell them something.

You are often not covered if you are doing something illegal. Even if every other tourist is hiring a motorbike in Thailand without a bike license, this doesn't mean that your medical bills will be paid if you hurt yourself. According to Thai law, you require a motorbike license to ride in Thailand, so your claim will probably get declined.

An accident which occurs when you are under the influence of illegal drugs will probably also not be covered.

DO YOUR HOMEWORK BEFORE LEAVING HOME

How can you stay safe when you travel and what can you do in advance?

PRE TRIP SKILLS

Learn some skills, at home, with access to proper instruction. Don't go snorkeling or boating if you can't swim. Go learn. Now. No, you don't have to be able to swim speeds or distances to see if you qualify for the Olympics. In fact my swimming is rubbish but I'm water confident. Get confident in water, in the sea, preferably, but a pool if nothing else. Make sure you can swim underwater as well as on top, learn to open your eyes underwater. Learn to duck dive and pick something up off the bottom. Really, it could save your life.

If you plan on a doing a lot of hiking, but normally take the car to the corner shops, do some local walking.

The worst that can happen is that you will break in the shoes that you are taking with you and get a bit fitter.

RESEARCH YOUR DESTINATION

Some countries have an unwarranted reputation for violence and danger. Others have entirely justified poor reputations. Generally, the bigger the city, regardless of the country, the more dangerous it can be for any number of reasons. There are bigger risks of theft, violence and getting hit crossing the road in New York than there are in a tiny country town in the mid-West. That's a universal rule for every country I've been to.

Poor countries aren't necessarily more or less safe than developed ones. Generally poor countries are less safe in terms of building standards and any form of public health and safety. Often, though, there is little violence, particularly toward tourists. Countries which are very dangerous for their own citizens who support concepts such as free speech or sympathizers who are journalists can be outstandingly safe for tourists. Why? Because the risk of being picked up by the police for a crime against a foreigner is basically a death sentence.

Read statistics with a bucket load of salt. Alice Springs in Australia's Northern Territory is Australia's murder capital but I can't find any reports of tourists being murdered. Unfortunately, it's all local on local violence in the Aborigine town camps.

Worldwide it's rare for tourists to be targeted – but it does happen, such as the well-publicized kidnappings of tourists (for money) by Yemeni pirates.

OFFICIAL TRAVEL ADVISORY SITES

I'd love to know the politics that see innocent little countries get tagged as dangerous when clearly they are not (e.g. Samoa), while other countries which have a serious amount of street crime (e.g. the US) are still rated as safe! Anyway, this is where you go for the "official" word on how dangerous your proposed itinerary actually is:

Australia: http://www.smartraveller.gov.au/

United Kingdom: http://www.fco.gov.uk/

United States: http://travel.state.gov/

The terminology varies between the three but they all have a "do-not travel" category. At the time of writing, out of the 200 odd countries in the world those three sites can agree on precisely five that you shouldn't go to:

- Afghanistan

- Mali

- Somalia

- Syria

- Yemen

Oddly, even Iraq doesn't make the list on all three; the UK has it in the next risk category down from 'don't go'! Really, it's a shooting war there! Fortunately, I don't think you'll find it very easy to get a tourist visa.

You should be aware that the list is highly political-the US has Iran on their "do not go" list, which is rather moot because Iran won't issue visas to Americans, anyway. America also has North Korea on their "do not go" list, while neither the UK nor Australia see it as particularly dangerous and an increasing number of tourists visit via organized tours from China.

Often, a lot of "warnings" come under the flipping obvious category. Both the UK and Australia flag Japan with the warning to avoid the radiation zone around the Fukushima Nuclear Power Plant (you'd need to get through the cordons first). According to the Australians, you should take great care around Christchurch, New Zealand, because of the 2011 earthquake. Fairly unclear about what the average tourist is supposed to do – all the non-earthquake resistant buildings have already fallen down, so, arguably, it's actually a lot safer than Wellington, which hasn't had a major earthquake for over 150 years. Plus, the no-go areas are securely fenced off…

Get a map out. For example Thailand is a large country but there is one small corner near the Malaysian border which has been off-limits to tourists for years, due to a local insurgency. That doesn't mean that visiting the rest of the country is the least bit dangerous, compared to, say, staying at home.

PACKING SENSIBLY

Don't pack to make yourself a target. Leave the family jewels, the expensive outfits or designer gear of any type at home. I've heard of people losing designer clothes from the hostel's washing line in Australia. My question is: why on earth would you travel with expensive designer jeans?

Prioritize: your passport, money and cards are important and need to be well looked after. Your electronics are nice to have but if they are desperately important to you, either insure them and take them or leave them at home.

Pack light. The more bags you are dragging around with you, the more risk you are at, particularly as you transfer from an airport. If you can easily carry everything yourself there is no legitimate reason for anyone else to ever need to lay a hand on your bags.

I don't always get to travel with carry-on bags only but I do when I am traveling for leisure. It's not particularly difficult to do and if you can cut your luggage down to under 10kg (22lbs) you'll find it all becomes a whole lot easier.

For more details about packing light - check out my book *The Non-Boring Vacation Packing Guide.*

YOU'RE NOT IN KANSAS NOW! PREPARING FOR CULTURE SHOCK

Culture shock is that feeling of something between bewilderment and fear that many people will get when they start traveling. It probably won't hit right away and sometimes it will hit when you return home, if you've been gone for a while.

WHAT IS CULTURE SHOCK?

You're an adult who knows how to find a cafe, catch local transit and order a meal. You understand the social mores of a shopping center; you know how to navigate a busy street. It's second nature. Then, you travel overseas and none of those rules apply. You expected to see new and wonderful sights. You kind of understood that you would stand out from the locals. You expected stuff to be different but you never expected that crossing the street could be such a huge challenge!

Or you may find that you are perfectly fine until something else happens – a minor theft, a cold, a missed connection – and then your reaction is entirely out of proportion to events. That's probably cultural shock.

Can you avoid it? Well I hope not! In fact, it's one of the great delights of traveling. Trying to buy ear drops in Homs, Syria turned out to be an adventure which has stuck more in my memory than some of the actual sights I have paid money to see.

Crossing the road in Vietnam was horrifying the first time, but hilarious by the tenth. You could accurately estimate how long a tourist had been in-country based on their ability to cross the road and how long they were prepared to wait for the traffic to stop (hint: it doesn't). Being unable to order from a menu most of the time has led me to discover dishes that, to this day, I still have no idea what they were, but I know they just tasted great!

So, pre-trip, what can you do to minimize culture shock? One of the real and practical difficulties is that the whole world doesn't speak English. Some places are worse than others. English didn't get me very far in Syria and South America forced me to learn Spanish. China stands apart as both having limited English outside of the main tourist spots and big cities, as well as a range of difficult languages to learn. On the other hand English is one of the national languages, in fact if not policy, for both India and the Philippines. In Samoa the taxi driver translated the radio sports news for us.

When words fail, though, you can still communicate. Smiling, eye contact, hand gestures – they are universal, right? Hmmm, actually, no. Looking someone in the eye, particularly an older person is downright rude in most of the Pacific. In much of Asia and the Pacific, you should never walk into a home with your shoes on. A shake of a head, which means "no" to most of us, traditionally means "yes" in Bulgaria, unless it's a younger person who may have adopted the Western meaning of the gesture i.e. "no"! Confused? You will be.

And somehow, it's worse when you think you share a common language. India comes top of many lists for the country most likely to induce culture shock in visitors, yet English is the most widely spoken language in the country. Every time I took a long distance train ride there was at least one other passenger nearby who could engage me in conversation fluently for hours and hours at a time. Usually, they knew more about the New Zealand cricket team than I did.

But, if you wanted it all to be the same - you'd stay home right? Globalization has had an effect, certainly, but the world is not and never will be, a homogeneous culture. Thank God.

DEALING WITH AND ENJOYING CULTURE SHOCK

So, what can you do to prepare for culture shock? First, know that it might happen. It may not, but being aware that it's a possibility, you may feel a huge desire to just stay in your hotel with your pillow over your head or spend eight hours straight in an Internet Cafe, means that you will recognize the symptoms.

Read. Get informed about the location you're going to. Buy or borrow guide books, check out the relevant Internet travel forums for the country. Know at least something of what to expect. If you are traveling for longer than a month and quite quickly and you start to get that disconnected feeling, I'd suggest that you are traveling too fast. Slow down and chill out.

PARLEZ VOUS FRANCAIS? HABLA ESPANOL?

If the language is going to be an issue, then consider whether you want to do something about it. It used to be completely the norm for any educated person in the West to speak several languages and read in more. It's still the norm in most non-Western countries. Now we have languages often in the "too hard basket". But, really, it's not that difficult. Again you don't need be fluent enough to defend a master's dissertation. You need a survival vocabulary.

A phrase book or a smartphone app will give you the basics:

- hello/goodbye/good morning/good evening

- thank you/please

- cheap/expensive

- Numbers and prices: if a coffee costs 2200 pesos, then learn how to say the numbers from 100 through 100,000. If the price is $2.20, learn the numbers from one to 100. Learn the common figures. Almost all the time, if the number is very important (e.g. when bargaining), the vendor will show you on a calculator. For small transactions, though, it is very useful to know what's being asked.

- arrive/depart

- bus/train/car/plane

- how much?

- where is?

- hotel room/restaurant/toilet/shop

- beer/red wine/white wine/ water/ carafe/ bottle/ glass/

- breakfast/lunch/dinner/meals

- close/far

- left/right/straight ahead

- 1st floor/ ground floor, etc.

- your nationality, country

- food/drink/menu/the bill(check)

- seat/reservation/1st class/2nd class

- if relevant: vegetarian/allergic to X, etc.

In fact some words you probably already know:

- Hotel
- Taxi
- WIFI *"weefee"*
- ATM
- Fone (telephone)
- WC

These are almost universal, though often pronounced differently, the English letters are often used even in countries where the alphabet is different.

MOST USEFUL LANGUAGES TO LEARN:

Spanish

I wouldn't say I'm fluent but after a couple of months of night classes plus six months of travel in South America, my travel Spanish is passable and even returns if I visit another Spanish-speaking country. For anyone spending significant time in Central (excluding Belize) or South America (excluding Brazil, Suriname, Guyana and French Guiana) or indeed Spain, it is well worth the effort.

Bahasa Indonesian/Malaysian

This is the official language of both countries, the second language in a lot of Indonesia and the first in Peninsular Malaysia. There is plenty of English spoken in Malaysia, but outside of Bali, you will find that you need Bahasa in Indonesia. It's a "trade language", which means it's designed to be spoken as a second language so it's pronounced as written and the grammar is very simple. There are a lot of Dutch borrowed words reflecting the colonial history of the region.

LANGUAGES WHICH USE SQUIGGLES FOR LETTERS

Focus on the numerals. Knowing the numerals from 1 to 10 in Arabic and Greek is very handy for handling coins and catching the right bus. It's not that hard to do. The Arabic numerals are what ours are based on, but are different enough.

HOW TO LEARN A LANGUAGE

Regardless if you enroll in class, buy a computer/audio course or buy a book you need to practice a language to improve. Keep a notebook and write things downs as you come across them and – study it – every night. Language learning is like learning math, science or a physical skill, such as dance. You can't go to lesson 1 and 2, skip 3 and 4 and expect to pick it all up at week 5. In fact enrolling in a class once a week is useless unless you study between lessons.

Learning through different media at the same time can be helpful e.g. taking a class *and* buying a DVD to study at home. The more you practice, the better you will get. Some people get it more quickly than others but anyone can learn a language if they really want to.

Once you have the basics - the trick is to just try. No one is going to refuse to serve you if you don't quite have the grammar right. "Please, beer two!" while standing at a bar, will work just as well as "Please, could I have two glasses of your draft lager"

Plan B: Learn to Speak English as a Second Language

Most of the time, you will find a local who will speak English as a second (or third, fourth, fifth) language. Most of the world is better at and more motivated to, learning English than we English native speakers are at learning theirs.

If they are doing you the courtesy of speaking English, do them a favor and make it easier for them. Don't speak LOUDER, speak slower. Drop the slang. Try to speak the version of English they are most familiar with. In South America that will be American English while in Europe it's more likely to be British English.

SUMMARY OF PART 1: PRE-TRIP PREPARATIONS

The short version for the attention-deficit afflicted among us:

- Do routine medical checks well in advance.

- Confirm and get the requisite vaccinations and boosters, also well in advance.

- Consider what medical suppliesyou need to carry with you (less is more).

- Ensure that you have the right travel health insurance coverage.

- Research your destination, but cross check and take government travel warnings with a boat-load of salt.

- Learn something about your destination and consider learning some of the language, if appropriate.

Part 2
Staying Healthy On The Road

"The greatest reward and luxury of travel is to be able to experience everyday things as if for the first time, to be in a position in which almost nothing is so familiar it is taken for granted."

—Bill Bryson

INTRODUCTION: STAYING HEALTHY ON THE ROAD

Right, so we finally left home! In this section I'll start with staying healthy on the road. You are far more likely to get food poisoning than to get robbed or raped while traveling.

Most people, when they think about staying healthy when traveling overseas, focus on food poisoning or exotic tropical diseases. The reality is rather more pragmatic. Travel insurance statistics suggest that for travelers over 50 the most common claim is related to heart issues. For younger travelers they are related to traffic accidents and other accidents associated with "adventure" activities.

Try this quick quiz: You wish to go bungee jumping, i.e. jumping off a tall structure with a rope tied around your feet. Which is likely to be the safest location? a) New Zealand b) Africa. The correct answer is New

Zealand. A very lucky Australian woman survived at 10+ meter fall at Victoria Falls, when the bungee cord was tied incorrectly, and nearly drowned.

Here's another one. Is it safe to float down a river which you are unfamiliar with, in an inner tube when heavily intoxicated and/or high on drugs, without a life jacket? Correct, if you said no. But there's a town which has built a tourist industry around just that: Vang Vieng, Laos. Just because everyone is doing it doesn't make it safe, particularly if you are new to drinking, drugs or tubing.

For many who live in the Western World, we are too used to living in a world of the Nanny State, which makes sure that everything we do is "safe". In the developing world, it's not quite the same. There are either no standards or standards are just dealt with by paying off the local officials. The onus is on you, as the consumer, to actually make a judgment call as to how safe this activity is and whether it's worth the risk. That said, I've seen people nearly die, because they just didn't know or understand the inherent risks in the country they were new to.

So this chapter has nothing to do with crimes against tourists and everything to do with how nature will try to get you.

FLYING AND JET LAG - WHAT TIME IS IT AGAIN?

For many of us overseas travel starts with a long flight. Those of us who live in New Zealand or Australia don't even count anything under eight hours as long! In an earlier era invalids were advised to take a sea voyage to improve their "constitution". I don't think anyone would advise you to take a long flight for your health's sake!

There are some tricks however, to minimize your health issues flying and it starts with booking the right flights.

FLIGHT PLANNING

The ideal flight is one that combines a great airline, spare seats, good airports en-route and the lowest price! It's not always possible but here are some things worth considering when trying to get the perfect combination.

Consider the day and time of flights. Flights are typically busy Monday mornings, Friday evenings and at "convenient times" which depart and arrive in daylight hours.

Consider if and where to break your journey. Any flight is better when broken up. A stop over will give you time to recover from jet lag, reduce the chance of DVT and of picking up a cold bug on the flight.

Often you will notice that your ticket is going to route you through an intermediate airport where you will have to change planes anyway, so consider if you would like to take advantage of this and spend a night or two.

IN THE AIR

Staying Hydrated

Modern jets fly with air pressures significantly lower than sea level. This can cause you to dehydrate quickly, which means alcohol will affect you more easily. The standard advice is to only drink soft drinks and water. However I find that a mixed drink, particularly a Bloody Mary, allows me to sleep without pills and doesn't dehydrate me too much.

Wear loose clothing and shoes that you will able to put back on if your feet swell during flight. For light sleepers you may find it useful to bring a blow up pillow and eye mask (the latter is sometimes handed out to passengers in flight).

Avoiding DVT

Deep vein thrombosis (DVT) can kill, from blood clots, caused by long periods of inactivity. In fact it's not restricted to air travel and has been diagnosed in passengers on long car or bus trips as well. Compression stockings or socks are recommended for anyone who has had recent surgery, poor circulation or heart conditions. Getting up and moving around the plane is a good idea too. Just avoid the times the seat belts signs are on for turbulence or when a meal service is in progress. You will feel better if you do some in-seat exercises, like leg raises. The in-flight magazine normally has some suggestions at the back.

Sleeping Pills

Many people swear by them, personally I don't use them. Why? Well frankly I'd rather minimize the risk of DVT and being out cold for a few hours is not a good way to do that. Also, I don't use them in real life, so starting to take them on a plane at 20,000 feet just seems silly, really. You may or may not sleep but there are worse things that can happen. If you're tired enough you will sleep, so if you are worried about not sleeping on the plane then don't get a good night's sleep before you leave and let nature do its thing.

East to West is best.

Flight direction matters. Crossing less than three time zones shouldn't affect most people too badly. Research suggests that the direction of travel also matters with westward flights, creating more jet lag for passengers than flights heading east. So maybe break up your westward leg with a stop-over to lessen the jet lag.

ON ARRIVAL

Give your body every opportunity to understand what time of day it is. If you arrive early in the morning, try to spend a lot of the day outside so that the brain can re-adjust to the shining sun! Finally, don't get too stressed about it. On a trip to Asia, I was wide awake at 5 a.m. Instead of lying in bed bored, I got up and explored Hanoi in the pre-dawn. It was a fascinating side of the city which would never have seen if I hadn't been jet lagged!

DELHI BELLY: OR WHEN FOOD STRIKES BACK!

Announcing that you are heading off to an exotic location for a few weeks will undoubtedly make you the recipient of much unsolicited advice on how to avoid Delhi Belly or Montezuma's Revenge.

Don't allow ice in your drinks! Don't eat from the food stalls! I have, in general, traveled cheap and eaten at local restaurants and street stalls. I love to eat and try new food; it's one of the reasons I travel. I like ice in my drinks and drink a lot of water. How often have I gotten sick? Five times, as far as I can remember. I mean in bed, on the toilet, can't think about leaving the room for between 12 hours and a couple of days, sick. One of those times was in Australia, another in Ireland – not exactly high risk countries. I've spent a total of four months traveling in India and didn't get ill at all.

Overall, I've more often gotten a bad cold when traveling than I have been affected by food poisoning.

WHEN IS IT FOOD POISONING?

Without being too gross, I want to describe what is and is not food poisoning. It's not having somewhat irregular bowel movements. That's probably more to do with your jet lag or with the complete change of diet, if you are used to eating very conservatively and consistently. All this is normal, to be expected and shouldn't really slow you down. If you can leave your hotel room without fear, you don't have serious food poisoning.If you eat something bad, you'll usually know within the hour, from one end of your digestive track or both.

If you feel it coming on, get back to your hotel room as soon as possible. If you have a shared bathroom, it might be a good time to upgrade to a private one! Now, and this is important, these symptoms can also mean that you have a serious disease, such as dysentery. If these symptoms persist for more than 48 hours and you're not getting better, seek medical attention. If you are passing blood, get medical help immediately.

WHY DO WE GET STOMACH UPSETS?

The food or the water always gets the blame, but it's not that simple. I've shared a meal with a friend who gave me the ice from his drink and his salad. He was in bed for two days, I was fine.

Why did I get violently ill after a birthday lunch at a very exclusive five-star restaurant in Ireland? I don't

61

think it was the food, as no one else was ill, I think it was my body. Lunch was a set lunch of four or five courses: it was traditional Irish cuisine, full of heavy cream sauces, excellent cheese and beautiful cream deserts. I usually have a filled roll for lunch. I was still a bit jet lagged, having flown half way around the world a few days earlier. I think my stomach objected to being over fed at a time, that my body still thought of as the middle of the night. Listen to your body; if it doesn't want to eat what's in front of you then don't eat it.

The next big culprit is often rancid cooking oil. It's hard to pick in advance, but I've been the victim of this in Australia, Vietnam and Bolivia. You can't identify it by smell or taste, basically all you can do is pick busy restaurants and stalls, who are more likely to have changed their oil recently.

TIPS TO AVOID FOOD POISONING

Eat where you can see the food being cooked. If the food is cooked in front of you and you eat it immediately, it's unlikely that you'll get sick. Don't assume that an expensive restaurant, where you can't see what's happening out back, is any safer than a food stall. It's not.

Eat where everyone else eats and eat what they are eating. Don't order tofu in a fish restaurant, as a friend of mine did. She got really ill, as the tofu had probably been in an unrefrigerated cupboard at the restaurant for longer than she'd been in Thailand!

Don't eat from the American or English menu, unless you happen to be in America or the UK. The locals don't know how to cook it and the ingredients will have been lying around for too long. Order what the locals are eating by pointing at nearby tables. If there is no one at the nearby tables, find another restaurant!

The bugs may not be in the food but they could have been on the plates and cutlery, which may have been rinsed in cold, dirty water. It's safer to accept food on paper plates or banana skins than on something that needs to be washed. Take your own plastic fork or throwaway chopsticks. Or, use your hands; there will almost always be a basin to wash your hands in a cheap restaurant and so long as you dry them well they should be reasonably sanitary. And, no, I don't carry hand sanitizer. It kills both good and bad bacteria and it's flammable. Soap and water is almost always available in restaurants of countries where the norm is to eat with your hands.

CHANGE YOUR DIET BEFORE LEAVING HOME

All you ever eat is three vegetables, meat and potatoes. You never eat chili, stir-fry, noodles or rice. You then fly to Asia for a two week vacation and start eating rice, noodles, tropical fruits and new spices two or three times a day. Do you think you will get an upset stomach? Probably. Is it food poisoning? No. You're just changing your eating habits suddenly and your digestive system is in shock. Try doing it at home: start eating out at an Indian or Thai restaurant twice a day for a week. Does your body react? Do you have food poisoning? Probably not, but you might feel a bit odd. Do a bit of trip preparation by varying your diet and eating the cuisine you are going to encounter overseas. It's nice thing to do to get into the spirit of travel anyway!

DRINK THE ICE AND WATER!

The ice in developing countries and the water are probably safer than the food! They are certainly safer than getting dehydrated! The ice is not made at the restaurant you are at, it's brought in from the ice plant, along with the drinking water. Everyone in the third world, who can afford to, drinks purified water and that's what they make the ice from. You will never be offered anything but purified water in a restaurant, no matter how cheap, even if it's just in an open jug. Restaurants know that tourists will demand water bottles with seals on them, so they will happily provide these, for a price, which is not to say that the water the locals are drinking is not good enough.

HOW TO RECOVER

If you have a stomach upset, diarrhea and are vomiting, watch for any of the following symptoms:

- Passing blood at either end.
- Vomiting for more than 48 hours.
- Very high fever, (i.e. shaking and chills).

- You're getting sicker and weaker over several days.

You may have something more serious than simple food poisoning such as gastroenteritis or dysentery. Get medical help. And I don't mean ask on the Internet. If you don't know where to find a doctor, find a pharmacy; they will be able to help or refer you to somewhere that can help. Or ask your hotel to call a doctor, they still make house calls in most non-Western countries. Some serious diseases are transmitted by contaminated food and water so make sure you have your vaccinations up to date for diseases including Typhoid and Hepatitis.

Far more likely, your main problem is avoiding dehydration particularly if it's hot. You need to keep drinking, even if you don't feel like it. In fact, you need to keep drinking particularly if you don't feel like it, because that's a symptom of dehydration. Avoid caffeine (energy drinks, coffee, tea), acidic drinks (fruit juices) and too much sugar. You probably won't want to drink anything too fizzy, so let soft drinks go flat. Diluted sports drinks are good and make sure you add some salt to replace the salts you're losing. You can also drink re-hydration mixture, which tastes nice and is designed to make sure you are getting the right electrolytes.

As you start to get better, don't throw too much at your abused digestive system in one go. Try eating bananas, apples, plain rice, plain bread, potato or yogurt. Eat a small amount and wait 30 minutes or so to see what happens (yes it's that quick). Obviously avoid fatty foods and meat until you are sure you're on the mend.

Do, however, keep eating, particularly if you've lost a lot of weight. Then you can get into a cycle of lethargy where you won't bother to eat, which basically means you are starving your body. No matter how attractive the thought of rapid weight loss is, it's not a healthy idea. Seriously.

WHAT NOT TO DO

You can buy plenty of products to stop diarrhea, but unless you MUST travel, it's not a good idea. You've been poisoned and your body is trying to expel whatever caused it, so don't take these remedies unless you have to. On the other hand, if you are faced with a long bus trip or a flight the following day taking Pepto-Bismol or Imodium makes sense; just don't continue taking it longer than is necessary.

WHY I DON'T CARRY ANTIBIOTICS

You may be offered or think you should take, antibiotics for stomach upsets. I don't carry them and here's why. First, they often will not work, against amoeba infection, such as giardia or dysentery.

But, worse than that, you are building up both your own immunity to the antibiotic you are taking (most commonly Cipro) and more seriously you are also making it more likely that the local bugs will also develop improved immunity. You are contributing to the worldwide problem of antibiotic resistance.

Plus, if you are already taking dioxcyclen or something similar for Malaria - that's already an antibiotic. If your food poisoning has not sorted itself out in a few days or is getting worse, seek medical advice, either by calling your insurance company's help line or from the locals.

HEAT: HOW TO SURVIVE IT

Go to a beach popular with the locals in Australia and what will you see on a hot summer's day? Lots of people wearing long sleeves and knee-length board shorts. In contrast, on the popular tourist beaches of Bondi and the Gold Coast you'll see skimpy Speedos, bikinis and pink, pink flesh.

In Australia's summer the UV-ray index is 11 (yes the scale used to be to 10, they upped it!) from 9:00 a.m. to after 4 p.m. The burn time is less than 10 minutes! So, what's the big deal you say? I get a little burned so what? Well, the short answer is skin cancer (a.k.a. melanoma). Oh and looking like a lined old woman or man before you hit 40!

There is an awful lot of nonsense written about what will give you cancer – everything from plastics to food has been accused of being carcinogenic – but one of the few absolutely proven links is between sunburn and melanoma.

Also, let's face it, a nasty case of sun burn can put you in the hospital. Third degree burns are crippling, painful and disfiguring, regardless of the source of the heat. You wouldn't deliberately burn yourself on a BBQ, why would you do it on a beach?

Where are you most at risk of sun burn?

- Countries that are under the ozone hole, which varies from year-to-year and with the seasons. Included are: Australia, New Zealand, southern Chile and southern Argentina. With the ozone hole you can even be burned on a cloudy day. These countries tend to have less air pollution in general, too.

- At the beach, especially a white-sand beach where the sand will better reflect the sun and effectively burn you twice.

- In the snow: again the snow reflects the UV-rays.

- High altitude: the air is thinner up there and gives less protection.

- On the water, thanks to the reflections.

TIPS FOR AVOIDING SUN DAMAGE ON YOUR VACATION

Stay out of the direct sun. As Noel Coward famously sang: "Only mad dogs and Englishmen go out in the midday sun". However, in hotter parts of the world the midday sun extends from 10 a.m. to 4 p.m.!

Cover up. The inhabitants of the Sahara Desert traditionally wear loose cotton clothes not just to protect themselves, covering up actually keeps you cooler in a dry hot climate and you don't dehydrate as quickly.

Wear a wide-brimmed hat, not just a baseball cap. Wear good quality sunglasses with large lenses and 100% UV-ray protection. Wear SPF 30 suntan lotion. Anything less that SPF 30 is a waste of time, according to the experts, anything more than SPF30 (you can buy up to SPF70 now) is a waste of money. The reason that Australians think the Irish and Scottish have lovely complexions is quite simple: the fair-skinned Celts, who haven't migrated from their homelands have very little sun damage to their skins!

WHAT IS SUN STROKE?

Sun stroke or heat stroke, is a serious medical condition which can kill you in a few hours. Basically, your body temperature goes over 40C (104F). Heat exhaustion is the less severe form. Symptoms include nausea, cramps, weakness and fatigue. Older people and children are most at risk but anyone who is doing a lot of exercise in a very hot and, particularly, a humid environment can suffer from it.

The treatment is the obvious of cooling the victim down: ice packs and getting them to drink cool liquids, if they are still capable of drinking. Seek medical help, quickly.

How to avoid it? Don't be stupid (i.e. don't jog in the middle of the day in a hot climate). And make sure you don't get dehydrated. That doesn't just mean drinking, it means the drinking right; no alcohol or caffeine (including caffeine-rich energy drinks) . And don't just drink water either, it's not enough in extreme conditions, particularly if you are not used to the climate. This is actually what Gatorade and similar "electrolytic energy drinks" are designed for. If you don't have any, add salt to fruit juice or anything else sweet. No, a hot drink won't "cool you down " (it's an old-wives' tale). There is a bit of a benefit to drinking iced liquids but don't drink them too quickly as they can cause cramps.

Are you are drinking enough? Here's an easy way to tell: if you are not peeing or if you are passing very dark yellow liquid, drink more – much more. Four liters (1 US gallon)/hour is quite normal.

FROSTBITE FOR BEGINNERS

Humans live in some very extreme temperatures. For cold weather, Canada comes immediately to mind. Not just any part of Canada, though. In fact, I thought I knew Canada's climate; I'd lived nearly a year in Vancouver (stop laughing NOW, Canucks). So, after Christmas, I caught a bus to Banff. It arrived at a reasonable hour – about 4 p.m. from memory but I'd forgotten that it would be dark by then. The bus had been nice and warm, but I figured it would be cold outside. So, I put my jacket on, before leaving the bus, but didn't zip it up. It was really cold. The driver gave me my pack and I realized I should probably put my hat and gloves on. I fumbled for my keys and by the time I was undoing the zip I was REALLY cold. It seemed like a good idea to do up my jacket's zip…

Now, I'm not saying that spending 15 minutes in –15C (5F) plus wind chill, put me in bed with the flu for the next couple of days, (meaning I've yet to see anything of Banff), but I don't think it helped. Frankly, I was lucky to not get frostbite – I'd barely got my pack re-zipped and all my clothing on, I was shaking so much.

DON'T UNDERESTIMATE THE TEMPERATURE

Here's the deal; if you live in a warm country you have no idea what cold is. If you live in a temperate country like the UK or South Africa you have no idea what REAL cold is like, say in Canada, inland US, China, Russia or Eastern Europe.

For example, I thought full-length winter coats, rather than hip length jackets, were just a fashion statement. Hmmm, no, not if it's seriously cold! Scarves aren't just a pretty accessory, the warm ones are essential if you don't want your face to fall off once the temperature is well below zero (Celsius, 32F).

DRESSING FOR THE COLD

So, how do you manage to not get hypothermia like I nearly did? Layers, it's old advice, but true. Wearing more, thinner layers in material like wool or Polypropylene will keep you warmer than one thick and chunky cotton or woolen layer. Why? Because the air trapped between the layers also acts as insulation. For the most severe conditions you need down or fur.

The trouble is that you often can't buy this type of gear before you arrive in the country. You haven't got a hope of buying clothing suitable for an European winter in Australia. Plus, of course, you may not actually need any of this clothing again. And unlike light-weight summer gear, it's often not cheap.

Here are some alternatives: first, second-hand shops. It can take a bit of time and may not work if you are a vastly different size from the locals, but it can be worth a look. Second, consider renting. I rented a lovely warm down jacket while hiking in Nepal and not only was it much cheaper than buying, I also didn't need to carry it during the warmer parts of the trek.

Finally, if you don't think you'll be able to buy what you need on arrival, consider some on-line shopping with Amazon or another online store before you leave home.

Even if you are leaving from a warm country, you should at least get lightweight thermal underwear and socks. Check out any shop which outfits campers or hikers. Even in Australia it can get cold in the desert in winter, so you will find some items in specialist camping stores.

NATURE DOESN'T COME WITH A HEALTH AND SAFETY GUARANTEE

I live in one of the world's more popular adventure playgrounds, New Zealand, and I regularly see news reports of tourists lucky to be alive. And, sometimes, they are not so lucky.

For a number of years, I lived in Australia. Again, tourists often died while hiking in remote areas–because they didn't understand the risks inherent to the combination of an extreme climate and the remoteness.

HIKING, GETTING LOST AND GETTING FOUND

I've been to National Parks in California too. I was amazed to be checked, on arrival, by park's staff – to ensure that I was carrying water in the vehicle! Of course I had water; I was driving in the desert! But apparently many tourists generally do believe that there is always a shop around the corner. If you are not familiar with outdoor hiking, even day walks, in your home country, then I suggest you do a few things before you try it overseas.

Get fit. This is the number one most important thing; if you are fitter you have a much better chance at survival and you're also more likely to have a good time. There is nothing more miserable than struggling to make the day's end point, I know!

Understand the climate you are going into and, particularly, the weather. If you are in mountainous regions, always be prepared regardless of the weather forecast. Fine and hot can turn into blizzard conditions inside half an hour and it often does.

Understand what the wildlife is and if it's dangerous. Be familiar with bears if you are hiking in Canada or parts of the US. Read up on crocodiles if you are camping in coastal parts of northern Australia.

Don't assume that a track is well sign posted. Getting lost is probably the most dangerous thing you can do in the wilderness. Find out just how well the track is marked. Consider hiring a guide. Take maps and know how to read them. No, I don't mean Google maps on your cell phone, which, incidentally, may very well not work in remote and mountainous regions. If you are in doubt, hire a personal locator beacon. If you get into a life-threatening situation you can activate the beacon and emergency services will come. There may or may not be a cost, depending on the country, but at least you'll be alive. While you are checking, read the fine print on your travel insurance policy. Make sure what you are doing is "hiking", which is generally covered, not "rock climbing" or "mountaineering" which may well not be.

ALTITUDE SICKNESS

High altitudes can kill you. Anything over 2400m (8000ft) can bring on altitude sickness, also known as *soroche* in South America. Ignore the symptoms and it can turn into the often fatal high altitude pulmonary edema (fluid in the lungs) or high altitude cerebral edema (swelling of the brain). The odd thing is that getting fit won't really help with this one. In fact, often, if you are hiking at altitude, it's the fittest people who get affected, because they go up too quickly.

Initially, the symptoms are pretty non-specific, a headache, lack of appetite, nausea, vomiting, insomnia, shortness of breath, nose bleeds, all of which could be anything from food poisoning to dehydration. In fact, the cold clear air at high altitude can often mean that you are also suffering from dehydration. Particularly with the cerebral edema, patients can become irrational as well. The most unhelpful advice is to avoid strenuous exercise when at high altitude. This might work if you are catching a bus over the Bolivian plateau or the Andes. It's not so useful if you are hiking or climbing.

If you are doing something strenuous, then the rule of thumb is quite simple. Above 2400m (8000ft) you shouldn't sleep more than 300m (1000ft) higher each night. So you can hike higher during the day, it's the altitude of your camp which matters. If you start getting symptoms, slow down. If they persist, go back down, wait a couple of days and try again. Almost everyone can eventually acclimatize – your body needs to catch up on the production of more red cells in your blood, so you can get sufficient oxygen from the lower amount in the air that you are breathing.

If someone with you starts showing serious symptoms, particularly if they are confused and argumentative, start walking them down, even if it's in the middle of the night. You might just save their life.

There seem to be few specific treatments for altitude sickness - you just need to get back to where there is more oxygen in the air. That will generally mean descending. The occasionally VERY fancy hotel at high altitude will have positive pressure oxygen rich rooms, but don't count on it.

DROWNING ON VACATION: DON'T LET THE WAVES WIN

Every year tourists die on the beaches of Thailand because they have no idea how to survive a rip on a surf beach. It's not just Thailand either, Australian beaches see tourist fatalities too.

It plays out like this: you book your perfect beach holiday. When you arrive at the beach and there are big waves, you think they look pretty cool and you see locals playing in them, so jump right in too. But, you haven't done a lot of swimming, except in a swimming pool or maybe a lake. The first wave catches you and dumps you, you roll over and over and you can't see the surface because: a) you don't like opening your eyes underwater or b) the sand in the water obscures the view. You finally get your head above water, you take a breath, between coughs, and then the next wave breaks over you.

Or, you decide to play it smart and decide to swim in the smooth channel you can see between the waves. No one else seems to be swimming there and the lifeguards are further up the beach. But it's logical that the smooth bit should be safe, right? You notice a surfer putting his board in at this spot and you make up your mind. The rip current starts to pull you out to sea. Un-nerved you start to swim back to shore, but you are going back-wards and you are now 20m off shore. You start to panic and you're tired because the current is so strong. It happened so fast.

How to Survive a Surf Beach

Both of those scenarios kill people each year but both are completely survivable.

The first rule is: don't panic. A rip is where the water flows away from the beach; it's a strong current and it moves around depending on the tide, the angle of the waves, the wind direction and a whole lot of other factors. A rip and this is important, doesn't go offshore very far. It stops at the back of the waves. If a rip takes you, all that will happen is that you end up behind the waves. That's why surfers use them as an easy way out to the back of the break.

So don't panic, let the current carry you out. Once you are out of the wave zone it's easy enough to float, signal for attention and get rescued.To avoid the rip in the first place, study how the waves are breaking before you enter the water. It's often incredibly easy to see rips, particularly from above, so if you are swimming on an un-patrolled beach, take a long look first.

If there are lifeguard flags on the beach then swim between them. If the flags are red then the beach is closed. These are international flag symbols which are consistent worldwide. Even if the beach is open swim between the flags. What, you don't want to swim with a crowd? How many guards are there? Two? Six? They are actively rescuing people, not just working on their tan. They can't watch the entire beach, only part of it, the bit between the flags.

If the beach is closed, that's sad on your holiday, but if you enter the water, get into trouble and have to be rescued, you've just not only risked your own life, but someone else's as well.

DIVING AND THE BENDS

There are plenty of dive schools looking to part your from your money for a dive certification course. It's worth checking if their credentials are internationally recognized (Google is your friend). Many will be employing someone who speaks your language as a native (dive master is one of the few qualifications which will get you a job in paradise), however, he or she may not have much actual experience past their qualification course.

One of the understated risks of diving in some countries, is the lack of a local hyperbaric chamber. If, for any reason, you end up with the bends (caused by coming up from depth too quickly), then treatment in a hyperbaric chamber can, in severe cases, be life-saving. Unfortunately you need access to that chamber within hours and emergency helicpter evacuation may, or may not be available. Plus you might want to make sure that your travel insurance will cover it.

RIVERS AND BOATS

Rivers and tubing, kayaking or rafting are also popular adventure sports. I got into trouble tubing in Sumatra, Indonesia. With a tube, instructions on where to get out to catch the bus back and a companion I'd met the night before, I headed out. I was in front and got caught on a bend. The current pushed me against a cliff, tipped me off the tube and then I couldn't get my head above water because of the strong downward current. Although it was clear and warm, I couldn't stand. I started to panic and basically climbed the cliff to get my head above water and then worked my way sideways out of the problem area. On the return to the hotel, I found that apparently I wasn't the first to have the problem in the same place. The solution was the same as with a surf rip, go with the flow and it would have popped me back up in the middle of the river and on the surface a few meters downstream.

Inner tubes are pretty hard to steer and if one side gets caught against or under anything, you will get flipped out. A life jacket would certainly have solved my problem, but these are often not available.

If you have no experience with kayaking and fast rivers, I'd try to get some experience before you try this out in the developing world. Again, there are a number of basic skills which you should have, for example, how to do a barrel roll and right your upturned kayak, while still in it. Kayaks on flat rivers and lakes are very safe, but on rivers with any type of rapids, you really should know the basics.

Rafts are larger and are normally piloted by someone who is, hopefully, competent. Again, though they do capsize, if you aren't happy being in the water at the very least make sure you do have a life jacket.

THINGS THAT DAMAGE HUMANS AND LIVE IN THE SEA

Coral reefs will not just cut you up badly, but often the corals are poisonous, so your cut will get infected. Healing infected cuts is a challenge in hot climates, particularly if you are in the water every day. Touching coral is a bad idea, both for the coral and you. If you are planning on diving or snorkeling from the shore on coral beaches, a pair of reef shoes are worth packing, if you don't have flippers with you. They will also protect you from sea urchin spines (poisonous, but easy to see) and stings from an assortment of wildlife, including stone fish (well camouflaged, rare and deadly) and cone shells (poisonous and under the sand, so invisible).

Sharks you may have heard of. But, fortunately, most sharks are harmless. You will most likely see small reef sharks if you dive or snorkel on or near, the seaward side of reefs. The headline shark attacks of great whites and other nasties almost invariably are of surfers, outside the wave break or fishermen, because the sharks are attracted by the fish guts thrown overboard.

I think the scariest thing I ever saw was on a pristine sandy beach in Papua New Guinea. We were camping in the area and had stopped to watch the wave breaks looking for rips, as there were no lifeguards on the island. We didn't see a rip, but we saw what we took to be large logs. Wondering how they got there, we watched a bit longer and realized that the "logs" were large salt water crocodiles. We didn't swim or camp nearby! Ask the locals and if they say it's risky, don't enter the beach, never mind the water. I prefer sharks; at least they can't chase you onto the sand!

Jelly fish can be a problem in some parts of the world. Sometimes in the tropics, you will come out of the water slightly itchy or even with a rash. I believe it's probably due to microscopic organisms or jellyfish larvae. Most jelly fish are okay, unless you are swimming in areas that have Box Jelly fish (northern Australia), which will kill even adults. If the beach is closed, it's for a very good reason.

There are often "stinger nets" set out for safe swimming. The treatment is common vinegar, buy some and keep it with you if you are traveling to remote beaches (town beaches will have vinegar available).

The pain is excruciating, but don't try to remove the tendrils instead, wash with vinegar (or any form of acetic acid) and seek medical attention.

SUMMARY PART 2: STAYING HEALTHY ON THE ROAD

The short version for the impatient:

- Jet lag is a given if you are flying across more than a couple of time zones. DVT, in contrast, is a serious risk for some travelers. Avoid.

- Most food poisoning is minor and all you need is rest and liquids. However, if it goes on too long, find a medical professional.

- The sun is a serious cause of cancer, plus getting burned hurts, a lot.

- Cold weather and altitude can get you, too.

- In the Great Outdoors you're responsible for your own safety. A cell phone does not equate to preparation.

- Drowning is one of the more common ways to die on vacation. Get water confident, and pack your common sense..

Part 3
Traveling Safely: Traffic, Petty Theft and Terrorism

"If you reject the food, ignore the customs, fear the religion and avoid the people, you might better stay at home."

—James Michener

INTRODUCTION: TRAVELING SAFELY; TRAFFIC, PETTY THEFT AND TERRORISM

Hopefully by now, I've given you some insight into the fact that trying new activities and disrespecting nature is far more likely to get you killed or hurt overseas than all the terrorists and bad guys out there.

However, the reality is, that when traveling we are more vulnerable than the average local. We stand out as a stranger, we are not comfortable with the local customs and language. We are carrying a passport and cards, which are highly inconvenient to lose. We are often perceived as being a lot richer than the locals and probably are.

It's still far more likely that you will be hurt in a traffic accident than that you will be seriously assaulted or attacked. Most theft is opportunistic and it's easy to remove most of the opportunities. Your chances of being assaulted is right up there with your risk of being caught up in a natural disaster. The most dangerous thing you'll do on holiday is get behind a vehicle's wheel or try to cross the road.

DRIVE TO SURVIVE: OR IMPROVE THE ODDS AND DON'T DRIVE

Driving overseas can be very different from driving at home! More tourists are injured in motor vehicle accidents, than from any other single cause according to official statistics. You may not even be driving, you might just be a passenger. But maybe this might make you think twice before you jump behind the wheel: many holiday makers under estimate the risk of driving in overseas cities and countries. It is a fairly common news story that a tourist has driven off the road and killed themselves or even more tragically pulled to the wrong side of the road and had a head on collision with someone coming the other way. Always driving at home doesn't equate to always driving on holiday.

Before you book a vehicle for your overseas trip, do some research. Not every destination is a good option for a self-drive holiday. Some places just have a whole different set of (sometimes unwritten) rules, as well as very different vehicles than you are used to. In many developing countries, it's unheard of to hire a car without a driver and that's because cars are valuable items and the owner doesn't want it damaged by an inexperienced tourist!

In other countries, it's safe to drive, but it might not make any sense. Plenty of Parisians would never think of driving around their home town, so why do you think, as a foreigner, it's a good idea? You'll struggle to find affordable or indeed any parking, spend a lot time lost, confused by the one-way street system and frustrated by your inability to find the sights you want to see.

Instead, you will see more and enjoy a much less stressful stay if you stick with public transport or hire a taxi for the day. In many European countries, it makes more sense to arrange to hire a vehicle, after you've explored the city and when you want to head in to the country, not on arrival.

DRIVING OVERSEAS TIPS

Don't drive jet-lagged. It can take days for your body's clock to get aligned with your destination's time zone. Do not push your luck and drive when you are still struggling to stay awake. In fact, don't drive tired, period. You are already dealing with an unfamiliar car in a strange town, so don't make it any more difficult.

Driving on the "wrong" side of the road is not too much of an issue in towns and cities where there are road marking and traffic to keep you on the correct side. However, it's a lot more difficult if the car is not designed for the side of the road you are driving on. So don't hire a right-hand drive car in the UK and then drive it in continental Europe. Cars are designed to have the driver in the middle of the road for a reason and you'll have very poor visibility driving with a car designed for the other side of the road.

Become familiar with local law variations; the most common variants, apart from speed limits, appears to be which of two vehicles turning into the same street give way and whether or not you can drive through a red light when turning.

Also, remember that, often, you will have to deal with a lot more animals on the road than you are used to. In fact in Outback Australia you'd be well advised to not drive at night at all until you are familiar with how to dodge wandering kangaroos and cattle.

Don't assume that the car you hire will be automatic. Plenty of countries still have many manual (stick shift) vehicles. If you can't drive a manual, then specify an automatic vehicle and expect to pay more for it.

Be particularly careful when riding a motorbike or scooter to not drift back to the "wrong" side of the road. There is no indication on the bike which side you should be on, so in light traffic it's easy to end up on the wrong side of the road, with potentially lethal consequences.

Whatever you are driving, slow down and drive ultra-defensively, it may just save your life and that of your passengers.

INTERNATIONAL OVERSEAS DRIVING PERMIT

If I haven't put you off entirely and you still intend to drive, then you may need some paperwork. Many countries, particularly non-English speaking ones, will require you to hold an International Driving Permit. These are issued by your home motoring association (AAA for Americans, AA for UK, your state organization for Australians).

Overseas permits don't replace your local license, which you should carry as well and they will cost you about $10 plus a photo.Make sure you get your permit endorsed for all the types of vehicles you are licensed for: typically this will be "B" for cars and "A" for motorbikes.International Permits aren't universally used. Some countries, for example the Cook Islands and Vietnam, will require you to buy a local license. The rental agency will do it for you or explain where to go.

OVERSEAS DRIVING INSURANCE

Make sure you understand what your travel insurance will and will not cover. For example, many foreigners will hire a motorbike to get around in Thailand. However, Thai law states that you need a full motorbike license to hire ANY motorbike in the

Kingdom. If you hire the bike and then have an accident (very common by the way), you will not only find that you are responsible for a few thousand dollars' worth of damage to the bike, but you may also find that your travel insurance will decline to cover your medical bills. That's because most travel insurance doesn't cover you when you are breaking the local laws.

Often in Australia and New Zealand, you will see very cheap rental car rates advertised. The fine print will tell you there is a $3000 deductible for any damage and you will be offered a policy to reduce this down to something more reasonable.

"No problem". You think. My travel insurance covers rental car damage. Well, many policies will only cover you, if you take all deductible reductions offered by the rental agency.

On the other hand, in some countries, vehicles are hired without any insurance being available, in which case it would be a good thing to already have some travel insurance which covers rental vehicle damage.

THEFT, PICKPOCKETING AND OTHER ANNOYANCES

Street theft is not as common as you think, as long as you don't walk around with a large virtual "victim" sign on you back. You are far more likely to get food poisoning or lose something by leaving it behind. Theft and assaults just make for better headlines.

Most tourists who have problems are victims of crime, not of violence. In fact, if you are from the US your chance of being murdered or otherwise seriously assaulted is much higher at home than it is overseas on vacation.

Almost all theft involving tourists is a sneak theft, slitting a bag while your back is turned or snatching it, picking your pocket or stealing from your hotel room while you are out.

The chance of being held at gun or knife point is very, very low. If that does, in fact, happen, then my advice is simple, give them whatever they want. It's just stuff and you probably have insurance; even if you don't, no jewelry or electronics are worth risking your life and health for.

HOW TO AVOID BECOMING A VICTIM

Travel Light

The less luggage you have, the easier it is to keep it close; simple, really. Grubby and old is a good look, too. And rip off the airline baggage tags before you leave the airport: they proclaim "I just got here!"

Don't leave bags unattended, ever. Not even for a millisecond. Don't sling a bag over the back of a chair particularly in a street-side or open-air cafe. If you are on the street with your luggage, you should be wearing it, either on your back or across your body. If you have more than two bags, you have a problem, because it just gets too hard to keep track of it all. Get a cab from the airport to the hotel and make sure that next time, you take less junk with you.

The Decoy Wallet Strategy

I have a crappy old wallet, which I use exclusively for travel. It looks as cheap as it was, has a couple of separate compartments useful for holding different currencies and that's about where its features ends. It's designed to be stolen; in fact, I wish someone would, but so far, I've had it for years. If someone is going to pickpocket you, (which is by far the most common form of theft) they are going to go for the obvious, easy item. That will be a wallet in a back pocket or anywhere else obvious, a bum bag, a camera bag slung over the back of your cafe chair, etc.

The thief can have my wallet, because it only ever has about a day's worth of local currency in it. And maybe one card, if that's what I'm using that day.Most of my cash, my other cards and particularly my passport, are not in a pocket. They are in a money belt worn next to my skin. No casual thief will find it or even notice it.

Another alternative is to dispense with a wallet entirely and just carry notes in a pocket. In most developing countries there are either no coins or the coins are of so little value you can safely ignore them. If you always have a pocket in your clothes, just carry the day's wad of cash in a pocket which buttons down or you can put a preferably dirty handkerchief over the top.

STAYING SAFE

At The Airport

Don't arrive after dark, particularly between midnight and dawn, after a long-haul flight, dis-orientated and jet lagged. Hey, it's a great rule, but sometimes airlines just don't play ball. If you have to arrive in the middle of the night then consider a couple of options. Stay at the airport, for free, if the airport is open 24 hours, they generally have good security. Or stay at a nearby hotel, which will often offer a free transfer. In these circumstances, I will book online from overseas. Beware that if you are arriving between midnight and midday and want a bed, you will need to book the night before (e.g. book the 12 July if you are arriving at 2a.m. 13 July) and ask for a late checkout!

At Your Hotel

Is your hotel room secure? Basically, no, even if the hotel has robust locks and a room safe, the staff still has access. If there is a criminal on the staff you may well have a problem. Frankly, this is far more a 3-star problem than a 5-star one, the more expensive the hotel, the more likely they have properly vetted and properly paid staff.

In cheaper hotels, what do you do make your room secure? Well, I take reasonable precautions without being paranoid. I do lock doors and screens before leaving and while sleeping, if there are locks. And, yes, plenty of times I've slept in places that have no locks. What do I do then? I keep desirable stuff (i.e. money and electronics), out of sight and out of reach of windows. I keep the valuable stuff in the bottom of my bag, under the dirty laundry.

If there is a safe in the room, I ignore it. Every hotel safe has someone with the master code. Some of them are fairly easy to unbolt and remove it entirely. Most hotels will also offer to hold your valuables at the desk; this often just means an unlocked drawer. Again, it's probably more risky than just wearing a money belt (fool proof) or hiding stuff at the bottom of your bag.

In cheap hotels, in the developing world, I've often had a room lock, which is just a padlock. I travel with a spare combination lock, sometimes with a short piece of chain and use this to replace their lock. You will also find, if staying in hostels, that there will often be lockers, so the lock will be useful there too. Whatever you do, do NOT take locks with keys; keys that can get lost. Instead have a couple of combination locks (TSA-approved if you are using them to lock checked luggage and flying via the US). The chain/lock combination, can also be handy for locking a pack to the top of a bus (a very common place for the luggage in South America and Africa) or onto to train luggage racks. Just make sure you know your combination and key all your locks to the same number. I find my year of birth is good enough.

On the Street

Take out the head phones and turn off your iPod. Being aware of your surroundings is important and using your sense of hearing is a part of that. It will also stop you from getting run over when you forget which side of the road the locals drive on. Look around you and make eye contact. If you are not used to walking around your home town you may not be familiar with just how much a vibe is obvious to the observant. It's called being street smart.

I've travelled many tens of thousands of miles and for many months as a solo woman and a blond to boot. I can remember just two times when I was nervous on the street and both were during daylight hours. Once was in San Francisco, the street was crowded, but everyone was just standing around, going nowhere. No one was making eye contact with me and I suddenly worried about just how many of those people were armed. Whether the fear was legitimate or not, I have no idea.

The second time was in a Brazilian border town near Iguassu Falls. I was walking down a street and I became aware that I was being followed. The area was notorious for petty theft. I tried to shake the person a couple of times by going into shops, but it didn't work. In the end I turned and walked back the way I came, made eye contact with my follower, a teenage boy, and greeted him in Portuguese. He took to his heels and ran, confirming my suspicions.

On Public Transit

In Paris recently, we struck snow delays, so when the metro came, it was very, very full. My wallet was in an inside pocket of a bag, which was across my body and under my arm. My partner's, though was visible in his front pocket. As we pushed onto the packed train, I warned him to watch his wallet. He put a hand in his pocket and felt someone else's trying to get into the same place. The wallet was actually in a zippered interior pocket, inside what looked like a conventional trouser pocket, so the wallet wasn't in danger, but my 60-something partner wasn't used to having other people's hands in his pockets! By the way neither of us could spot the thief even though we were standing next to each other. They are that good.

Beware of the pick pocket hot spots. It varies over time, but here's a few popular spots:

- Taj Mahal, India. I lost some rupees from a wallet on the train to the Taj Mahal and not one person I told about it was even slightly surprised.

- Tourist attractions in Europe, particularly where there are crowds. The good news is that if you are even slightly aware and protective of your belongings, you will be a less easy mark than the next tourist and the thief will move on.

- Packed buses and trains anywhere near a tourist hot spot, particularly in Europe and, to a lesser extent, large Asian cities.

Don't take out your expensive smartphone or other expensive electronics and hold it loosely in your hand, on the edge of the footpath within reach of anyone on the back of a motorbike.

Don't allow yourself to be distracted. The old tricks still work, the guy who volunteers to help you with your luggage on the train or bus, who then takes off with it or passes it to a mate.

Be suspicious of someone helping you to clean the mess on your shoulder from the pigeon, his mate is slitting your bag or picking your back pocket

Put nothing more important than a street map in your back pocket or the outside pocket of your day bag.

Be careful using ATMs. I much prefer to use the ones inside banks or at least in a mall or store, rather than on the open street. It makes it harder for you to be observed and followed.

Don't ever wave wads of cash around in places like markets; this should be obvious, but apparently it's not. Don't show off that you are wearing a money belt and have lots of cash in it. Never use your money belt in public; if you have to retrieve more money from it, find a changing room or WC and do it in private.

If you think you are being followed, then stop, turn and go back way you came. The follower will probably flee. If you need to, go into a shop or restaurant, where people running a legitimate business who are unlikely to want you to be hassled on their premises.

But the biggest risk on the street isn't losing your money; it's getting bowled over by the crazy traffic in many countries. I once went out at dawn for a walk along the Mekong River in Phnom Penh, Cambodia. It was quiet and beautiful. But, by the time I got back several hours later the town was well and truly awake and I had a problem, getting back to my hotel. I could see it: on the opposite side of the wide, French-designed, boulevard. Originally, I imagine, the road was made for four lanes of traffic, except now there were a varying number of lanes of traffic, maybe six or eight, depending. It was chaotic and fast-moving and there was no hope of a break in the traffic. I watched the locals; as they crossed the road, so I decided that I was going to cross, by shadowing an elderly woman. After all she hadn't died in a traffic accident, yet. But she was too quick for me and halfway across I got separated from her and ended up shadowing a couple of kids of about eight years old. I finally got to the other side and the kids turned round and had a huge laugh that they had just helped an adult cross the road!

In A Business

Getting short-changed with businesses is not unknown. However, before you start yelling, make sure they are just not rounding up the price. The price may be 1990 pesos for a coke; you are likely to be charged 2000, as no one will have a 10 peso coin. This even happens in countries such as New Zealand and Australia, where the smallest denomination is a 10 cent coin, but prices are still quoted to the cent. You'll only be charged the exact price if you pay by card.

The most common way of getting significantly short-changed is when you change money, particularly on the street with an un-official vendor. It's less common than it used to be, thanks to the world-wide spread of the ATM, but it does still happen, particularly at land border crossings. Either avoid the touts completely or change a minimal amount.

It's much safer to change either at a bank or a jewelry shop. In this circumstance it's far easier to check you change. Do so, even if it's going to take a while. And reject any very dirty notes.

Out On The Town

Getting totally pissed/wasted/plastered particularly with new "friends" is a high risk strategy. Even at home. Maybe it's because I'm a woman, but I don't ever

103

get totally out of control when I'm traveling solo. And I've met men who wish they hadn't either. When I'm traveling with a companion, we decide who is going to be the "sober driver" at the start of the evening, even if there is no vehicle involved.

Spiking drinks is not just a developed country scam. If you are in a common pick up joint, remember the bartender may be an accomplice.

You can have the most secure money belt in the world. You can have a careful decoy wallet, but bring your new "friend" back to your hotel, lock the door and yes your possessions may leave with her. (Yes I know it's possible for women to hire escorts in some parts of the world, but to be blunt I'm talking about the 99% here which are men picking up local women).

If you are going out drinking then that is probably one time I would leave my valuables in the hotel safe or stashed in my room.

And never bring people you just met back to your room. If you want to have casual sex, then go to a different hotel and book it by the hour, she'll know where to go.

LOCAL TRANSPORT: PLAYING SARDINES FOR GROWN-UPS

Local transportation will range from the astoundingly good to the astonishingly bad, with pretty much anything in between.

The use or not, of local transportation is pretty much what will separate the organized tourist from the independent traveler. Plenty of tourists will never consider using local transport; instead making sure that their hotel provides transfers from location to location, with a private driver or coach thrown in for the sightseeing.

The independent traveler, though, may venture further afield and actually look around, to see how the locals get from place to place. Now, in many countries of the first world, the answer is, of course, their car. America is not the only country with a love affair with the car. In Australia, Canada and New Zealand, you will find an awful lot of locals who never catch a bus. In Europe maybe slightly more so, but getting around Ireland or Scotland without transport can be extremely challenging.

The exception is, big cities. It's no accident that New York and San Francisco, even in car-obsessed America, have great public transport. Any major European city will have a great system too.

So, in much of the world, if you are not using private transfers and drivers, you will be using the local transportation.

RIVER BOATS

Getting rarer by the year, river transport is probably the safest form of surface transport, particularly because the countries that still have viable river transport systems (Myanmar, Cambodia, Laos etc.) have neglected the rest of their transport infrastructure for years. Basically, if something will float on a river, it will probably keep floating. There is a reason that river transport tends to either die out or remain as a "tourist excursion", it's very, very slow. So, take lots of food, water and sun block just in case the trip takes a day or two longer than expected.

Rating: low risk, but often very slow.

OCEAN GOING CRAFT

Many other countries have plenty of ferry options. Developed countries, where locals want to take their vehicles along, will often have cheap ferries including

Canada, Europe and Chile. Less developed countries will have them too. Traveling in the Pacific or South East Asia means that you will end up on a local ferries.

More likely than not, these will be just fine. However, ferries do get over-loaded and sail in bad weather conditions when they shouldn't. I remember being frustrated for days in Rhodes, Greece, because the ferries weren't leaving port. However, from a safety point of view, it was probably a good thing considering the poor weather that some local boat operators will sail in through places like Fiji, Indonesia and the Philippines, all of which have seen boats going down with fatalities. A random Google search reveals maybe 200 dead after a Bangladesh ferry sinks, a 100 lost on a sunken Papua New Guinea ferry and dozens dead after a Tongan ferry sunk. None of these which made the headlines like the cruise ship "Costa Concordia" sinking in the Mediterranean.

Ratings: moderate, you need to make a call when you see the boat. How to make a judgment? The biggest risk of a boat going down–is being trapped in it. I once spent a very scary night on the deck of a tiny ferry crossing the Straits of Malacca, from Indonesia to Singapore. I was worried about going over the side, there were no real rails around the edge but I wouldn't go below decks, where the locals were because, I, at least, wanted to have a chance as we threaded between huge super-tankers, who wouldn't have even known if they had hit and destroyed us. The biggest risk with boats is the weather. An unsafe boat will be fine, until the weather turns bad. Operators won't cancel, like that Greek port master, because they make no money if they don't sail.

Just remember the weather will generally be worse out of the port, not better. At the end of the day, you choose to board or not.

BUSES AND MINI-VANS

Bus crashes can happen anywhere; recently, there have been bad crashes in Switzerland and Australia. However, I would take a bus in either of those countries, without a second thought; their road standards, vehicle licensing regulations and driver training are as good as it gets. You'll almost certainly be safer in a large, modern bus with a qualified and experienced driver than you would be driving your own small vehicle. Again, most crashes don't make the news.

If you have the choice, then a larger bus is probably safer than a mini-van, purely because they can't go as fast and the lower the speed at impact, the better your survival chances. It's always a good idea to not sit right in the front, too; halfway the aisle is perfect, avoid the very back (past the rear axle) because that can be the bumpiest spot. I've come off buses sporting very large bruises just from being thrown around inside, no accident required!

TRAINS

Trains are my land transport of choice, normally. The bus will usually beat a train, but a train has some big advantages. They tend to leave from and arrive in the center of town, not in some distant bus station. They have more leg room than the bus, are easier to get up and walk around, minimizing the risk of DVT and they are much safer. The standard laws of physics apply to all moving objects; the heaviest, slowest moving vehicle will come off best. Trains are generally pretty slow, with the obvious exception of the new super-fast networks of Europe, Japan and China. A slow local train, may derail or even collide, but your chances of survival, are excellent because: a) the chances of this is much lower on a controlled (even haphazardly) railroad than a random road and b) derailment at 20km an hour will probably see you walk out without a bruise.

TAXIS/RICKSHAWS/MOTOS/CYCLOS

Taxis can be interesting, not just because of the crazy driving, but also because you are vulnerable to the driver. Taxis taken you somewhere remote and then robbing you is not unheard of in some countries in South America.

In most countries vehicles are often unregulated and un-metered. You will need to negotiate the fare up-front and I'd rate Taxis as the most likely place to be seriously over-charged as a foreigner.

In busy cities with a decent rail network, taxis aren't even the fastest option to get around!

To minimize the risk of taxis I'd use official stands at airports and get your hotel to arrange one, rather than just stopping a random vehicle on the street.

Often in Asia and elsewhere you will come across motorcycles being used as taxis. Bikes can look like a normal bike. You ride pillion and the driver will put your bag in front of him (a good time to be traveling light). You should hang onto the back of the bike not around the drivers waist. Often though, the bike is the basis for a 3-wheeled vehicle called a "moto" or "tuk tuk". Motos are slower than a taxi and often no cheaper, but can be a lot easier to exit in hurry, if you need to.

Rarely, you will still come across man-powered rickshaws (the bicycle version of a moto). Obviously, these are significantly more dangerous than motorized options, as they offer no protection if you collide with anything bigger and heavier(i.e. everything else on the road). Rickshaws are pretty much disappearing now, even from countries such as Vietnam and India, where they used to be common. But, actually, I like them. They're slow and obviously dangerous, but they're definitely great to sightsee from.

Oh and seat belts and child seats? Nowhere outside the western world will provide these or if they do, they will be decorative only.

THEFT ON TRANSPORT

Buses and trains are both easy places to lose luggage, so, again, being alert is important. There are some country specific scams that you should know about in advance. The large buses of Thailand seem to specialize in having people crawl through the luggage in the cargo area, knowing that they have hours to check the contents of the bags. I travel with a pack which has zips I can lock together and I never leave electronics in a bag I've checked in on any form of transport. If you are traveling with carry-on only, then it's easy: just keep your bag with you, inside the bus.

Another problem is long trips on trains, which tend to have a lot of people getting on and off and moving through. Bags can also go walkabout or get slashed if under the seat. In South America I bought a short goat chain and used that to attach my pack to the rack. A determined thief would still have gotten it, all they needed was a sharp knife to cut my strap, but most of this type of security is just making it that much harder to steal than the next one. And it meant I could get up and go the dining car or to the WC without worrying.And a quick word about pacsafes: these are high on my "use less travel gear" list. A pacsafe is a heavy metal mesh which you pull over the top of your pack to advertise: "Steal me, I have valuables inside".

They are heavy and expensive and using one means that the thief will take the whole pack rather than slitting the bag. There is a much easier way to deal with this anywhere you are worried about bag slashers. In any outside pockets, put things like laundry or your towel or maps and other tourist brochures you may have picked up.

THE REALLY UNLIKELY STUFF: EARTHQUAKES, TSUNAMIS AND TERRORISTS

Yes the news in the headlines? It hardly every happens in real life. Really if you genuinely think that you are likely to fall victim to earthquakes, tsunamis or terrorists, I suggest you buy your lottery ticket now!

WHEN THE GROUND MOVES FOR YOU

Building Standards and Earthquake Survival

The single most important factor for surviving an earthquake is the quality of the building you are in. A building which complies to stringent earthquake standards will save your life. During a shake, extraneous material such as shelving and ceiling tiles will collapse and make a big mess. But the roof will stay up for quite a long time. If the entire building does collapse then it will create big gaps in the rubble, gaps which will protect you and probably trap you, but not kill you.

The tragedy of the 2008 Sichuan, China, earthquake was not the earthquake itself, but the abysmal building standards which saw thousands killed under collapsed buildings. The same happened at L'Aquila, Italy, the 500 year-old medieval buildings survived, as they have through other earthquakes, but the apartments built in the 1960's did not.

HOW TO SURVIVE AN EARTHQUAKE

Run Outside an Unsafe Building

Decide whether the building you are in is safe. When I worked for a geotechnical engineer in Wellington, our office was one of the buildings that, at the time, was considered completely unsafe. It was an unreinforced brick warehouse on reclaimed land and we were on the first floor in an open plan office. The earthquake plan was simple: sprint for the stairs and throw yourself down them. Seriously. The stairwell is the most likely structure to survive. Move fast though, as the shaking increases you won't be able to stand never mind run.

I would use this principle for any building in countries that "don't have" earthquakes such as Australia. Also use this in countries like Mexico and China, who demonstrably don't have building standards or none that are actually complied to, anyway.

Stay Inside a Safe Building

By the way, this is the official advice from authorities: get under a desk and hold onto the legs. The desk will move, but you need to go with it. Or sit down in a doorway and brace yourself, always protecting your head. Unless there is fire, stay there. The first earthquake may be the first of several; a quake can last one minute or up to five, the next shake can be within two or three minutes or many hours later.

KILLER WAVE - TSUNAMIS

Until the memory of Japan's horrific 2011 tsunami fades along with the 2004 Boxing Day tsunami which killed tens of thousands in Thailand/Indonesia/India, it's probably safe to say that a lot more people are aware of tsunamis than they used to be. In fact, on a recent trip to Samoa, which had a nasty tsunami in 2009, I was told by a survivor that they knew to run for the hills because of the TV footage of the 2004 wave.

A tsunami is a wave created by an under-sea landslide, which in turn is usually caused by an earthquake. The earthquake may have been quite minor; in fact, the earthquake that caused the 2009 Samoa tsunami wasn't even noticed by many people.

Best Places to Survive a Tsunami

Out at sea: after the Boxing Day tsunami there were reports of villages in Indonesia that had lost most of their women, children and elderly, all of whom were in the village when the wave struck. The men, away fishing on boats, survived. Tourists diving off Thailand's Andaman coast surfaced, because visibility reduced to the point that they could see nothing underwater. They didn't even notice the wave and had no idea of the wide-spread destruction on shore.

The tsunami wave only builds as it approaches shore, where there is less depth to the water. That's why a tsunami's damage is so hard to predict.

If you aren't lucky enough to be at sea, the second best place to be is inland. If you see something odd at sea, do not go to the beach to film it! Stay inland and go higher if you can.

If you're on the beach or the nearby coastal plain, then you are at risk.

Getting higher is better than nothing (a multi-story building or even a coconut tree). Do not take your bag or even your passport with you. Run, do not walk, in whatever you're wearing, away from the sea.

Don't wait for the water to retreat: if you feel a strong earthquake, near the sea, run for high ground. If you do see the water start to retreat unusually, even if you didn't feel the earthquake, run for high ground.

Subsequent waves may be higher. Just because the first one wasn't bad, doesn't mean the next one won't be worse.

If you end up in the water, chances are that you will get sucked out to sea and will drown. Try to avoid getting in the water at all costs.

WHAT HAPPENS AFTER A NATURAL DISASTER?

Well. universally, the first response of the local authorities is to remove tourists from the affected area. They are a drain on resources and need to leave. After Christchurch's earthquake in 2011, the first planes out of the city carried tourists who were moved to other New Zealand cities. They were then issued temporary passports if required.

In fact, a large scale natural disaster is the one time when losing your passport isn't really that big of a problem. Your embassy and local authorities will facilitate your paper work. You may not get your luggage back for a while, if ever. In the case of Christchurch, many tourists had bags left in hotel rooms, which although not destroyed in the quake, were behind cordons for months. In some cases, luggage was returned up to a year later!

TERRORISM AND KIDNAPPING

I've left the least likely to last: terrorism, including hijacking, kidnappings, bombing and other random acts of violence. They make great headlines, but the reality is that if tourists get hurt, they are generally collateral damage, not the target of the bad guys.

If you are seriously worried about being targeted by terrorists, there is a very simple solution: avoid staying in well-known prominent hotels in capital cities. No one goes around bombing youth hostels!

I lived in London during part of the decades-long IRA bombing campaign and I quickly learned to be suspicious of any parcel or bag left unattended, particularly on public transport. The outcome was, that there were no longer any luggage lockers at major UK train stations and leaving a bag alone at an airport was more likely to get it blown up, rather than stolen. This was in the 1980's, the perception is that the world has got more dangerous since 9/11, but it hasn't.

The reality is that you may get incredibly unlucky and get caught in the cross-fire or you may win the lotto. Your lotto odds are a lot better, as are your chances of getting run overlooking the wrong way on the street or misplacing your luggage.

Terrorism is really not worth worrying about. An asteroid may hit the Earth and destroy all life and you have no control over that either.

PART 3 SUMMARY: TRAVELING SAFELY: TRAFFIC, PETTY THEFT AND TERRORISM

The short version, for those who jumped straight here:

- Pretty much, staying safe and unmolested when traveling is simply a matter of being slightly better prepared and aware than the tourist next to you. In the unlikely event of a pickpocket coming after your bling, your best defensive is a) to have no bling and b) to be very aware of what is happening around you.

- This goes treble if you are venturing on to a new country's roads. Be the ultra-defensive driver, hire a local, take a bus or ride the train.

- Most theft will happen fast and is not violent. However it's pretty easy to minimize the risks, stay alert and don't wander around in a drunken stupor.

119

- Local transport can be fun. Or not. Either way, be alert to what is happening around you and keep your bags close.

- Natural disasters can happen. But rarely, very, very rarely. Worry about the traffic instead.

- As the ancient Mayans believed that the world will end in 2012, maybe we should just skip the paranoia about terrorism, okay?

Afterword
When Going Home Feels Wrong

"The whole object of travel is not to set foot on foreign land; it is at last to set foot on one's own country as a foreign land."

– G. K. Chesterton

ILLNESSES YOU MAY HAVE PICKED UP

If you end up ill within a couple of weeks of returning home, make sure your doctor knows where you've been. A couple died of malaria in New Zealand, a few years ago. They got sick in a small town, in a country that has never seen malaria and, by the time their symptoms were recognized and they were transferred to the country's only tropical diseases unit, it was too late.

Be careful if you are happy to be finally back driving on the "right" side of the road. After a year of living in Canada and driving on the "wrong" side, I relaxed in London and immediately got run over by a black cab, which I stepped out straight in front of, because I looked the wrong way!

POST TRAVEL BLUES

I doubt you will find a medical practitioner that will diagnose this strange malady, but as a repeat sufferer I can tell you what it looks like:

- dis-orientation: everything is strange, because it's familiar. You realize that when you are walking down the street, no one looks twice at you.

- you wake up every morning and then remember where you are and feel sad.

- you try to explain to friends and family why walking the Inca Trail or the highlights of Northern Thailand are cool and no one cares.

- they don't want to see your photos, either.

What can you do about it? Well, first off, I suggest you don't confide in your friends; particularly the ones that don't travel. You've just come back from vacation and you're sad. Sympathy will be in short supply.

I genuinely thought that once I returned home, broke, from my first six-month long backpacking trip through Asia, I'd be 'cured'. Yeah, right. About as cured as an alcoholic is cured after they've been on a six-month-long drinking binge. You may feel hung over (broke) for a while, but cured, no.

Travel is an addiction and for some of us there is no known cure. Not everyone gets addicted. In the same way I can take or leave booze, some people can do a trip or maybe two and then be quite content to stay home, decorate and procreate.

For some of us there is no known cure. I had an aunt who explored Outer Mongolia in her 80's. If you can't lose that feeling that there is something else to see out there, then frankly, there is only one solution to that nagging feeling that you need to be elsewhere. Start saving and planning for your next trip.

There's a reason that most bookshops have a large armchair travel section. You will find your fellow addicts there or online at the travel forums and blogs that litter the Internet.

ABOUT THE AUTHOR

Elisabeth has been traveling since she was seven. Her mother was ill and in the days before dads could look after their kids, she was packed off to a holiday in Ireland with relatives. Elisabeth doesn't remember the trip, but she does remember the excitement of catching her first flight, unaccompanied! These days Elisabeth finds airports and long-haul flights as exciting as a wet Sunday, but she still loves showing up at the airport for the start of a new travel adventure.

Elisabeth has traveled to every continent except Antarctica and that's on the list. She has traveled solo, with friends and with her partner. She's stayed in hostels the fleas weren't impressed with and luxury resorts. She has seen the travel industry evolve from the days before Internet when the only information on a remote destination was a guide book years out of date, to today's twitter-driven instant feedback, well-connected online experience. She's not convinced that this is all good.

These days Elisabeth writes in the back bedroom, in New Zealand's capital city Wellington, with easy access to the airport and the world. Elisabeth is a writer, developer and promoter of websites about various topics, but travel is still her passion.

The Non-Boring Travel Guides series is her attempt to share her love and knowledge of travel with the world.

A REQUEST FROM THE AUTHOR

I hope you have enjoyed *The Non-Boring Safe Travel Guide*. If you've got a minute I'd really appreciate it if you left an honest review of it at Amazon.com. Book reviews help other readers decide on the books they love and it would mean a lot to me.

Thank you, Elisabeth

FREE UPDATES TO THIS BOOK

Want to keep up to date? Things change, sometimes things go bad, often then improve. Fortunately these days it's easy to update books! If you want to get those updates for FREE, including any new versions of this book I'll publish, please go here and sign-up.

http://NonBoringTravelGuides.com/STBonus

FROM THE SAME AUTHOR

THE NON-BORING VACATION PACKING GUIDE

SAVE YOUR BACK, TIME AND MONEY

Packing – how hard can it be? The person who asks that – probably has his partner do the vacation packing!

Should you take a ball gown with you on a backpacking trip of Canada?

Can you buy swimsuits in Thailand?

What happens if you forget to pack your prescription meds for a trip to Costa Rica?

Yes these are all real questions that can be found on any forum discussing vacation travel!

The premise of this book is simple: figure out why you want to over-pack, decide what you need to pack, then pack and go!

Rather than hundreds of pages of all-purpose packing lists for every conceivable type of trip and traveler, this book explains how you can create your own customized list – a list of gear that you will actually use on your trip.

Having too much luggage has its advantages, though. Do you want to come back home after a trip with great looking arms? All those over-head lifts of your bag into luggage racks will be great, plus you should get some nice quads from dragging bags up and down stairs, in and out of hotels, planes and autos. If you want your luggage to provide you with a gym fix, don't buy this book.

If you'd like to have a low-stress vacation, you should buy it.

What? Another Book About Packing?

Most packing books seem intent on selling you a new set of luggage. This one is different – this one is about the "why" of packing, and in particular over-packing. The author uses the science of why you think you need 25 different outfits for a 10 day beach vacation, to kill your over-packing habit once and for all.

Of course you can skip the book and take what you think you need for the next vacation. But do you really want to spend the entire trip counting bags in and out of taxis, hotels and planes? Do you enjoy paying porters and tipping taxi drivers to deal with your stuff?

Available now at Amazon.com and other online retailors.

Or buy direct from the author at

www.NonBoringTravelGuides.com

Printed in Great Britain
by Amazon

28508007R00076